JavaScript Enlightenment

Cody Lindley

 O'REILLY®

Beijing · Cambridge · Farnham · Köln · Sebastopol · Tokyo

JavaScript Enlightenment

by Cody Lindley

Printed in the United States of America.

Published by O'Reilly Media, Inc., 1005 Gravenstein Highway North, Sebastopol, CA 95472.

O'Reilly books may be purchased for educational, business, or sales promotional use. Online editions are also available for most titles (*http://my.safaribooksonline.com*). For more information, contact our corporate/institutional sales department: 800-998-9938 or *corporate@oreilly.com*.

Editors: Simon St. Laurent and Meghan Blanchette	**Proofreader:** BIM Proofreading Services
Production Editor: Kristen Borg	**Indexer:** Ellen Troutman Zaig
	Cover Designer: Randy Comer
	Interior Designer: David Futato

January 2013:   First Edition

Revision History for the First Edition:

2012-12-18   First release

See *http://oreilly.com/catalog/errata.csp?isbn=9781449342883* for release details.

ISBN: 978-1-449-34288-3

[LSI]

Table of Contents

Preface

Introduction

This book is not about JavaScript design patterns or implementing an object-oriented paradigm with JavaScript code. It was not written to distinguish the good features of the JavaScript language from the bad. It is not meant to be a complete reference guide. It is not targeted at people new to programming or those completely new to JavaScript. Nor is this a cookbook of JavaScript recipes. Those books have been written.

It was my intention to write a book to give the reader an accurate JavaScript worldview through an examination of native JavaScript objects and supporting nuances: complex values, primitive values, scope, inheritance, the head object, etc. I intend this book to be a short and digestible summary of the ECMAScript 3 Edition specification, focused on the nature of objects in JavaScript.

If you are a designer or developer who has only used JavaScript under the mantle of libraries (such as jQuery, MooTools, Zepto, YUI, Dojo, etc.), it is my hope that the material in this book will transform you from a JavaScript library user into a JavaScript developer.

Why Did I Write This Book?

First, I must admit that I wrote this book for myself. Truth be told, I crafted this material so I could drink my own Kool-Aid and always remember what it tastes like. In other words, I wanted a reference written in my own words used to jog my memory as needed. Additionally:

- Libraries facilitate a "black box" syndrome that can be beneficial in some regards, but detrimental in others. Things may get done fast and efficiently, but you have no idea how or why. And the how and why really matter when things go wrong or performance becomes an issue. The fact is that anyone who intends to implement a JavaScript library or framework when building a web application (or just a good signup form) ought to look under the hood and understand the engine. This book was written for those who want to pop the hood and get their hands dirty in Java-Script itself.

- Mozilla has provided the most up-to-date and complete reference guide for Java-Script 1.5. I believe what is missing is a digestible document, written from a single point of view, to go along with their reference guide. It is my hope that this book will serve as a "what you need to know" manual for JavaScript values, detailing concepts beyond what the Mozilla reference covers.

- Version 1.5 of JavaScript is going to be around for a fair amount of time, but as we move towards the new additions to the language found in ES5 and ES6, I wanted to document the cornerstone concepts of JavaScript that will likely be perennial.

- Advanced technical books written about programing languages are often full of monolithic code examples and pointless meanderings. I prefer short explanations that get to the point, backed by real code that I can run instantly. I coined a term, "technical thin-slicing," to describe what I am attempting to employ in this book. This entails reducing complex topics into smaller, digestible concepts taught with minimal words and backed with comprehensive/focused code examples.

- Most JavaScript books worth reading are three inches thick. Definitive guides like David Flanigan's certainly have their place, but I wanted to create a book that hones in on the important stuff without being exhaustive.

Who Should Read This Book?

This book is targeted at two types of people. The first is an advanced beginner or in-termediate JavaScript developer who wishes to solidify his or her understanding of the language through an in-depth look at JavaScript objects. The second type is a JavaScript library veteran who is ready to look behind the curtain. This book is not ideal for newbies to programming, JavaScript libraries, or JavaScript itself.

Why JavaScript 1.5 and ECMAScript 3 Edition?

In this book, I focus on version 1.5 of JavaScript (equivalent to ECMAScript 3 Edition) because it is the most widely implemented version of JavaScript to date. The next version of this book will certainly be geared towards the up-and-coming ES5 and ES6.

Why Didn't I Cover the Date(), Error(), and RegEx() Objects?

Like I said, this book is not an exhaustive reference guide to JavaScript. Rather, it focuses on objects as a lens through which to understand JavaScript. So I have decided not to cover the Date(), Error(), or RegEx() objects because, as useful as they are, grasping the details of these objects will not make or break your general understanding of objects in JavaScript. My hope is that you simply apply what you learn here to all objects available in the JavaScript environment.

Before you begin, it is important to understand various styles employed in this book. Please do not skip this section, because it contains important information that will aid you as you read the book.

More Code, Fewer Words

Please examine the code examples in detail. The text should be viewed as secondary to the code itself. It is my opinion that a code example is worth a thousand words. Do not worry if you're initially confused by explanations. Examine the code. Tinker with it. Reread the code comments. Repeat this process until the concept being explained becomes clear. I hope you achieve a level of expertise such that well-documented code is all you need to grok a programming concept.

Exhaustive Code and Repetition

You will probably curse me for repeating myself and for being so comprehensive with my code examples. And while I might deserve it, I prefer to err on the side of being exact, verbose, and repetitive, rather than make false assumptions authors often make about their reader. Yes, both can be annoying, depending upon what knowledge you bring to the subject, but they can also serve a useful purpose for those who want to learn a subject in detail.

Color-Coding Conventions

In the JavaScript code examples (example shown below), bold is used to highlight code directly relevant to the concept being discussed. Any additional code used to support the bold code will be in normal text. The lighter gray in the code examples is reserved for JavaScript comments (example shown below).

```
<!DOCTYPE html><html lang="en"><body><script>

// this is a comment about a specific part of the code
var foo = 'calling out this part of the code';

</script></body></html>
```

jsFiddle, JS Bin, and Firebug lite-dev

The majority of code examples in this book are linked to a corresponding jsFiddle page (*http://jsfiddle.net/*), where the code can be tweaked and executed online. The jsFiddle examples have been configured to use the Firebug lite-dev plugin (*http://fbug.googlecode.com/svn/lite/branches/firebug1.3/content/firebug-lite-dev.js*) so that the log function (i.e., `console.log`) will work in most any modern browser regardless of whether the browser has its own console. Before reading this book, make sure you are comfortable with the usage and purpose of `console.log` (*http://stackoverflow.com/questions/4743730/javascript-what-is-console-log-and-how-do-i-use-it*).

In situations where jsFiddle and Firebug lite-dev caused complications with the Java-Script code JS Bin (*http://jsbin.tumblr.com/about*) and Firebug Lite-dev will be used. I've tried to avoid a dependency on a browser console by using Firebug lite-dev but with certain code examples the solution itself gets in the way of code execution. In these situations the console built into your web browser will have to be leveraged to output logs. If you are not using a browser with a built-in JavaScript console, I would suggest upgrading or switching browsers (*http://browsehappy.com/*).

When JS Bin is used, keep in mind that the code has to be executed manually (clicking "Render"), which differs from the page load execution done by jsFiddle.

Conventions Used in This Book

The following typographical conventions are used in this book [see also "Color-Coding Conventions" (page xi)]:

Italic
> Indicates new terms, URLs, email addresses, filenames, and file extensions.

`Constant width`
> Used for program listings, as well as within paragraphs to refer to program elements such as variable or function names, databases, data types, environment variables, statements, and keywords.

`Constant width bold`
> Shows commands or other text that should be typed literally by the user.

`Constant width italic`
> Shows text that should be replaced with user-supplied values or by values determined by context.

 This icon signifies a tip, suggestion, or general note.

This icon indicates a warning or caution.

Using Code Examples

This book is here to help you get your job done. In general, if this book includes code examples, you may use the code in your programs and documentation. You do not need to contact us for permission unless you're reproducing a significant portion of the code. For example, writing a program that uses several chunks of code from this book does not require permission. Selling or distributing a CD-ROM of examples from O'Reilly books does require permission. Answering a question by citing this book and quoting example code does not require permission. Incorporating a significant amount of example code from this book into your product's documentation does require permission.

We appreciate, but do not require, attribution. An attribution usually includes the title, author, publisher, and ISBN. For example: "*JavaScript Enlightenment* by Cody Lindley (O'Reilly). Copyright 2013 Cody Lindley, 978-1-449-34288-3."

If you feel your use of code examples falls outside fair use or the permission given above, feel free to contact us at *permissions@oreilly.com*.

Safari® Books Online

 Safari Books Online (*www.safaribooksonline.com*) is an on-demand digital library that delivers expert content in both book and video form from the world's leading authors in technology and business.

Technology professionals, software developers, web designers, and business and creative professionals use Safari Books Online as their primary resource for research, problem solving, learning, and certification training.

Safari Books Online offers a range of product mixes and pricing programs for organizations, government agencies, and individuals. Subscribers have access to thousands of books, training videos, and prepublication manuscripts in one fully searchable database from publishers like O'Reilly Media, Prentice Hall Professional, Addison-Wesley Professional, Microsoft Press, Sams, Que, Peachpit Press, Focal Press, Cisco Press, John Wiley & Sons, Syngress, Morgan Kaufmann, IBM Redbooks, Packt, Adobe Press, FT Press, Apress, Manning, New Riders, McGraw-Hill, Jones & Bartlett, Course Technology, and dozens more. For more information about Safari Books Online, please visit us online.

How to Contact Us

Please address comments and questions concerning this book to the publisher:

O'Reilly Media, Inc.
1005 Gravenstein Highway North
Sebastopol, CA 95472
800-998-9938 (in the United States or Canada)
707-829-0515 (international or local)
707-829-0104 (fax)

We have a web page for this book, where we list errata, examples, and any additional information. You can access this page at *http://oreil.ly/javascript_enlightenment*.

To comment or ask technical questions about this book, send email to *bookquestions@oreilly.com*.

For more information about our books, courses, conferences, and news, see our website at *http://www.oreilly.com*.

Find us on Facebook: *http://facebook.com/oreilly*

Follow us on Twitter: *http://twitter.com/oreillymedia*

Watch us on YouTube: *http://www.youtube.com/oreillymedia*

About the Author

Cody Lindley is a client-side engineer (a.k.a. front-end developer) and recovering Flash developer. He has an extensive background working professionally (11+ years) with HTML, CSS, JavaScript, Flash, and client-side performance techniques as it pertains to web development. If he is not wielding client-side code, he is likely toying with interface/interaction design or authoring material and speaking at various conferences. When not sitting in front of a computer, it is a sure bet he is hanging out with his wife and kids in Boise, Idaho—training for triathlons, skiing, mountain biking, road biking, alpine climbing, reading, watching movies, or debating the rational evidence for a Christian worldview.

About the Technical Editors

Michael Richardson

Michael Richardson is a web and application developer living in Boise, Idaho. Way back when, he got an MFA in creative writing from Sarah Lawrence and published a novel in 2003 called Plans for a Mushroom Radio. These days, when he's not spending quality time with his lovely wife and rascal kid, he's managing his little web-based application called Timeglider (*http://timeglider.com/*).

Kyle Simpson

Kyle Simpson is a JavaScript Systems Architect from Austin, Texas. He focuses on JavaScript, web performance optimization, and "middle-end" application architecture. If something can't be done in JavaScript or web stack technology, he's probably bored by it. He runs several open-source projects, including *LABjs*, HandlebarJS (*http://handlebarjs.com/*), and BikechainJS (*http://bikechainjs.com/*). Kyle works as a Software Engineer on the Development Tools team for Mozilla.

Nathan Smith

Nathan Smith (*http://sonspring.com*) is a UX developer at HP. He holds a MDiv from Asbury Theological Seminary. He began building sites late last century and enjoys hand coding HTML, CSS, and JavaScript. He created the 960 Grid System (*http://960.gs/*), a design and CSS framework for sketching, designing, and coding page layouts. He also made Formalize (*http://formalize.me*), a JavaScript and CSS framework that endeavors to bring sanity to form styling.

Ben Nadel

Ben Nadel is the chief software engineer at Epicenter Consulting, a Manhattan-based web application development firm specializing in innovative custom software that transforms the way its clients do business. He is also an Adobe Community Professional as well as an Adobe Certified Professional in Advanced ColdFusion. In his spare time, he blogs extensively about all aspects of obsessively thorough web application development at *www.bennadel.com*.

Ryan Florence

Ryan Florence (*http://ryanflorence.com/*) is a front-end web developer from Salt Lake City, Utah, and has been creating websites since the early 90's. He is especially interested in creating experiences that are pleasing to both the end user and the developer inheriting the project. Ryan is active in the JavaScript community writing plugins, contributing to popular JavaScript libraries, speaking at conferences and meet-ups, and writing about it on the web. He currently works as a Senior Technical Consultant at Clock Four.

Nathan Logan

Nathan Logan (*http://nathanlogan.com/*) has been a professional web developer for eight years. His focus is on client-side technologies, but he also digs the server-side. He currently works for Memolane, alongside the author of this book. Personally, Nathan is blessed with a wonderful wife and son, and enjoys mountain biking, hot springs, spicy food, scotch, and Christian faith/theology.

CHAPTER 1

JavaScript Objects

Creating Objects

In JavaScript, objects are king: Almost everything is an object or acts like an object. Understand objects and you will understand JavaScript. So let's examine the creation of objects in JavaScript.

An object is just a container for a collection of named values (a.k.a. properties). Before we look at any JavaScript code, let's first reason this out. Take myself, for example. Using plain language, we can express in a table, a "cody":

	cody
property:	property value:
living	true
age	33
gender	male

The word "cody" in the table above is just a label for the group of property names and corresponding values that make up exactly what a cody is. As you can see from the table, I am living, 33, and a male.

JavaScript, however, does not speak in tables. It speaks in objects, which are not unlike the parts contained in the "cody" table. Translating the above table into an actual JavaScript object would look like this:

Live Code (*http://jsfiddle.net/javascriptenlightenment/ckVA5/*)

```
<!DOCTYPE html><html lang="en"><body><script>

// create the cody object...
var cody = new Object();
```

```
// then fill the cody object with properties (using dot notation)
cody.living = true;
cody.age = 33;
cody.gender = 'male';

console.log(cody); // logs Object {living = true, age = 33, gender = 'male'}

</script></body></html>
```

Keep this at the forefront of your mind: objects are really just containers for properties, each of which has a name and a value. This notion of a container of properties with named values (i.e., an object) is used by JavaScript as the building blocks for expressing values in JavaScript. The cody object is a value which I expressed as a JavaScript object by creating an object, giving the object a name, and then giving the object properties.

Up to this point, the cody object we are discussing has only static information. Since we are dealing with a programing language, we want to program our cody object to actually do something. Otherwise, all we really have is a database, akin to JSON (*http://www.json.org/*). In order to bring the cody object to life, I need to add a property *method*. Property methods perform a function. To be precise (*http://bclary.com/2004/11/07/%23a-4.3.3*), in JavaScript, methods are properties that contain a Function() object, whose intent is to operate on the object the function is contained within.

If I were to update the cody table with a getGender method, in plain English it would look like this:

cody	
property:	property value:
living	true
age	33
gender	male
getGender	return the value of gender

Using JavaScript, the getGender method from the updated "cody" table above would look like this:

Live Code (*http://jsfiddle.net/javascriptenlightenment/3gBT4/*)

```
<!DOCTYPE html><html lang="en"><body><script>

var cody = new Object();
cody.living = true;
cody.age = 33;
cody.gender = 'male';
cody.getGender = function(){return cody.gender;};
```

```
console.log(cody.getGender()); // logs 'male'

</script></body></html>
```

The getGender method, a property of the cody object, is used to return one of cody's other property values: the value "male" stored in the gender property. What you must realize is that without methods, our object would not do much except store static properties.

The cody object we have discussed thus far is what is known as an Object() object. We created the cody object using a blank object that was provided to us by invoking the Object() constructor function. Think of constructor functions as a template or cookie cutter for producing pre-defined objects. In the case of the cody object, I used the Object() constructor function to produce an empty object which I named cody. Now since cody is an object constructed from the Object() constructor, we call cody an Object() object. What you really need to grok, beyond the creation of a simple Object() object like cody, is that the majority of values expressed in JavaScript are objects (primitive values like "foo", 5, and true are the exception but have equivalent wrapper objects).

Consider that the cody object created from the Object() constructor function is not really different from, say, a string object created via the String() constructor function. To drive this fact home, examine and contrast the code below:

Live Code (*http://jsfiddle.net/javascriptenlightenment/XcfC5/*)

```
<!DOCTYPE html><html lang="en"><body><script>

var myObject = new Object(); // produces an Object() object
myObject['0'] = 'f';
myObject['1'] = 'o';
myObject['2'] = 'o';

console.log(myObject); // logs Object { 0="f", 1="o", 2="o"}

var myString = new String('foo'); // produces a String() object

console.log(myString); // logs foo { 0="f", 1="o", 2="o"}

</script></body></html>
```

As it turns out, myObject and myString are both…objects! They both can have properties, inherit properties, and are produced from a constructor function. The myString variable containing the 'foo' string value seems to be as simple as it goes, but amazingly it's got an object structure under its surface. If you examine both of the objects produced, you will see that they are identical objects in substance but not in type. More importantly, I hope you begin to see that JavaScript uses objects to express values.

Note

You might find it odd to see the string value 'foo' in the object form because typically a string is represented in JavaScript as a primitive value (e.g., var myString = 'foo';). I specifically used a string object value here to highlight that anything can be an object, including values that we might not typically think of as an object (i.e., string, number, boolean). Also, I think this helps explain why some say that everything in JavaScript can be an object.

JavaScript bakes the String() and Object() constructor functions into the language itself to make the creation of a String() object and Object() object trivial. But you, as a coder of the JavaScript language, can also create equally powerful constructor functions. Below, I demonstrate this by defining a non-native custom Person() constructor function, so that I can create people from it.

Live Code (*http://jsfiddle.net/javascriptenlightenment/zQDSw/*)

```
<!DOCTYPE html><html lang="en"><body><script>

/* define Person constructor function in order to create custom
Person() objects later */
var Person = function(living, age, gender) {
   this.living = living;
   this.age = age;
   this.gender = gender;
   this.getGender = function() {return this.gender;};
};

// instantiate a Person object and store it in the cody variable
var cody = new Person(true, 33, 'male');

console.log(cody);

/* The String() constructor function below, having been defined by JavaScript,
has the same pattern. Because the string constructor is native to JavaScript,
all we have to do to get a string instance is instantiate it. But the pattern is
the same whether we use native constructors like String() or user-defined
constructors like Person(). */

// instantiate a String object stored in the myString variable
var myString = new String('foo');

console.log(myString);

</script></body></html>
```

The user-defined Person() constructor function can produce person objects, just as the native String() constructor function can produce string objects. The Person() constructor is no less capable, and is no more or less malleable, than the native String() constructor or any of the native constructors found in JavaScript.

Remember how the cody object we first looked at was produced from an Object(). It's important to note that the Object() constructor function and the new Person() constructor shown in the last code example can give us identical outcomes. Both can produce an identical object with the same properties and property methods. Examine the two sections of code below, showing that codyA and codyB have the same object values, even though they are produced in different ways.

Live Code (*http://jsfiddle.net/javascriptenlightenment/Du5YV/*)

```
<!DOCTYPE html><html lang="en"><body><script>

// create a codyA object using the Object() constructor

var codyA = new Object();
codyA.living = true;
codyA.age = 33;
codyA.gender = 'male';
codyA.getGender = function() {return codyA.gender;};

console.log(codyA); // logs Object {living=true, age=33, gender="male", ...}

/* The same cody object is created below, but instead of using the native
Object() constructor to create a one-off cody, we first define our own Person()
constructor that can create a cody object (and any other Person object we like)
and then instantiate it with "new". */

var Person = function(living, age, gender) {
   this.living = living;
   this.age = age;
   this.gender = gender;
   this.getGender = function() {return this.gender;};
};

// logs Object {living=true, age=33, gender="male", ...}
var codyB = new Person(true, 33, 'male');

console.log(codyB);

</script></body></html>
```

The main difference between the codyA and codyB objects is not found in the object itself, but in the constructor functions used to produce the objects. The codyA object was produced using an instance of the `Object()` constructor. The `Person()` constructor constructed codyB but can also be used as a powerful, centrally defined object "factory" to be used for creating more `Person()` objects. Crafting your own constructors for producing custom objects also sets up prototypal inheritance for `Person()` instances.

Both solutions resulted in the same complex object being created. It's these two patterns that are the most commonly used for constructing objects.

JavaScript is really just a language that is pre-packaged with a few native object constructors used to produce complex objects which express a very specific type of value (e.g., numbers, strings, functions, object, arrays, etc.), as well as the raw materials via `Function()` objects for crafting user-defined object constructors [e.g., `Person()`]. The end result—no matter the pattern for creating the object—is typically the creation of a complex object.

Understanding the creation, nature, and usage of objects and their primitive equivalents is the focus of the rest of this book.

JavaScript Constructors Construct and Return Object Instances

The role of a constructor function is to create multiple objects that share certain qualities and behaviors. Basically a constructor function is a cookie cutter for producing objects that have default properties and property methods.

If you said, "A constructor is nothing more than a function," then I would reply, "You are correct—unless that function is invoked using the new keyword." [e.g., `new String('foo')`]. When this happens, a function takes on a special role, and JavaScript treats the function as special by setting the value of this for the function to the new object that is being constructed. In addition to this special behavior, the function will return the newly created object (i.e., this) by default instead of a falsey value. The new object that is returned from the function is considered to be an instance of the constructor function that constructs it.

Consider the `Person()` constructor again, but this time read the comments in the code below carefully, as they highlight the effect of the new keyword.

Live Code (*http://jsfiddle.net/javascriptenlightenment/YPR6Q/*)

```
<!DOCTYPE html><html lang="en"><body><script>

/* Person is a constructor function. It was written with the intent of being used
with the new keyword. */

var Person = function Person(living, age, gender) {
    /* "this" below is the new object that is being created
       (i.e., this = new Object();) */
```

```
    this.living = living;
    this.age = age;
    this.gender = gender;
    this.getGender = function() {return this.gender;};
    /* when the function is called with the new keyword "this" is returned
    instead of undefined */
};

// instantiate a Person object named cody
var cody = new Person(true, 33, 'male');

// cody is an object and an instance of Person()
console.log(typeof cody); // logs object
console.log(cody); // logs the internal properties and values of cody
console.log(cody.constructor); // logs the Person() function

</script></body></html>
```

The above code leverages a user-defined constructor function [i.e., `Person()`] to create the cody object. This is no different from the `Array()` constructor creating an `Array()` object [e.g., `new Array()`]:

Live Code (http://jsfiddle.net/javascriptenlightenment/cKa3a/)

```
<!DOCTYPE html><html lang="en"><body><script>

// instantiate an Array object named myArray
var myArray = new Array(); // myArray is an instance of Array

// myArray is an object and an instance of Array() constructor
console.log(typeof myArray); // logs object! What? Yes, arrays are type of object

console.log(myArray); // logs [ ]

console.log(myArray.constructor); // logs Array()

</script></body></html>
```

In JavaScript, most values (excluding primitive values) involve objects being created, or *instantiated*, from a constructor function. An object returned from a constructor is called an *instance*. Make sure you are comfortable with these semantics, as well as the pattern of leveraging constructors to construct objects.

The JavaScript Native/Built-In Object Constructors

The JavaScript language contains nine native (or built-in) object constructors. These objects are used by JavaScript to construct the language, and by "construct" I mean that these objects are used to express object values in JavaScript code, as well as orchestrate several features of the language. Thus, the native object constructors are multifaceted in that they produce objects, but are also leveraged in facilitating many of the language's programming conventions. For example, functions are objects created from the Function() constructor, but are also used to create other objects when called as constructor functions using the new keyword.

Below, I list the nine native object constructors that come pre-packaged with JavaScript:

- Number()
- String()
- Boolean()
- Object()
- Array()
- Function()
- Date()
- RegExp()
- Error()

JavaScript is mostly constructed from just these nine objects (as well as string, number, and boolean primitive values). Understanding these objects in detail is key to taking advantage of JavaScript's unique programming power and language flexibility.

Notes

- The Math object is the oddball here. It's a static object, rather than a constructor function, meaning you can't do this: var x = new Math(). But you can use it as if it has already been instantiated (e.g., Math.PI). Truly, Math is a just an object namespace set up by Java-Script to house math functions.

- The native objects are sometimes referred to as "global objects" since they are the objects that JavaScript has made natively available for use. Do not confuse the term *global object* with the "head" global object that is the topmost level of the scope chain, for example, the window object in all web browsers.

- The Number(), String(), and Boolean() constructors not only construct objects; they also provide a primitive value for a string, number and boolean, depending upon how the constructor is leveraged. If you called these constructors directly, then a complex object is returned. If you simply express a number, string, or boolean value in your code (primitive values like 5, "foo" and true), then the constructor will return a primitive value instead of a complex object value.

User-Defined/Non-Native Object Constructor Functions

As you saw with the Person() constructor, we can make our own constructor functions, from which we can produce not just one but *multiple* custom objects.

Below, I present the familiar Person() constructor function:

Live Code (*http://jsfiddle.net/javascriptenlightenment/GLMr8/*)

```
<!DOCTYPE html><html lang="en"><body><script>

var Person = function(living, age, gender) {
    this.living = living;
    this.age = age;
    this.gender = gender;
    this.getGender = function() {return this.gender;};
};

var cody = new Person(true, 33, 'male');
console.log(cody); // logs Object {living=true, age=33, gender="male", ...}

var lisa = new Person(true, 34, 'female');
console.log(lisa); // logs Object {living=true, age=34, gender="female", ...}

</script></body></html>
```

As you can see, by passing unique parameters and invoking the `Person()` constructor function, you could easily create a vast number of unique people objects. This can be pretty handy when you need more than two or three objects that possess the same properties, but with different values. Come to think of it, this is exactly what JavaScript does with the native objects. The `Person()` constructor follows the same principles as the `Array()` constructor. So `new Array('foo','bar')` is really not that different than `new Person(true, 33, 'male')`. Creating your own constructor functions is just using the same pattern that JavaScript itself uses for its own native constructor functions.

 Notes

- It is not required, but when creating custom constructor functions intended to be used with the new operator, it's best practice to make the first character of the constructor name uppercase: `Person()` rather than `person()`.

- One tricky thing about constructor functions is the use of the `this` value inside of the function. Remember, a constructor function is just a cookie cutter. When used with the new keyword, it will create an object with properties and values defined inside of the constructor function. When new is used, the value `this` literally means the new object/instance that will be created based on the statements inside the constructor function. On the other hand, if you create a constructor function and call it without the use of the new keyword the `this` value will refer to the "parent" object that contains the function. More detail about this topic can be found in Chapter 6.

- It's possible to forgo the use of the new keyword and the concept of a constructor function by explicitly having the function return an object. The function would have to be written explicitly to build an `Object()` object and return it: `var myFunction = function() {return {prop: val}};`. Doing this, however, sidesteps prototypal inheritance.

Instantiating Constructors Using the new Operator

A constructor function is basically a cookie cutter template used to create pre-configured objects. Take `String()` for example. This function, when used with the new operator [`new String('foo')`] creates a string instance based on the `String()` "template." Let's look at an example.

Live Code (*http://jsfiddle.net/javascriptenlightenment/FKdsp/*)

```
<!DOCTYPE html><html lang="en"><body><script>

var myString = new String('foo');
```

```
console.log(myString); // logs foo {0 = "f", 1 = "o", 2 = "o"}

</script></body></html>
```

Above, we created a new string object that is an instance of the `String()` constructor function. Just like that, we have a string value expressed in JavaScript.

Note

I'm not suggesting that you use constructor functions instead of their literal/primitive equivalents—like var `string="foo";`. I am, however, suggesting that you understand what is going on behind literal/primitive values.

As previously mentioned, the JavaScript language has the following native predefined constructors: `Number()`, `String()`, `Boolean()`, `Object()`, `Array()`, `Function()`, `Date()`, `RegExp()`, and `Error()`. We can instantiate an object instance from any of these constructor functions by applying the new operator. Below, I construct these nine native JavaScript objects.

Live Code (*http://jsfiddle.net/javascriptenlightenment/M9cWA/*)

```
<!DOCTYPE html><html lang="en"><body><script>

// instantiate an instance for each native constructor using the new keyword

var myNumber = new Number(23);
var myString = new String('male');
var myBoolean = new Boolean(false);
var myObject = new Object();
var myArray = new Array('foo','bar');
var myFunction = new Function("x", "y", "return x*y");
var myDate = new Date();
var myRegExp = new RegExp('\bt[a-z]+\b');
var myError = new Error('Crap!');

// log/verify which constructor created the object
console.log(myNumber.constructor); // logs Number()
console.log(myString.constructor); // logs String()
console.log(myBoolean.constructor); // logs Boolean()
console.log(myObject.constructor); // logs Object()
console.log(myArray.constructor); //logs Array(), in modern browsers
console.log(myFunction.constructor); // logs Function()
console.log(myDate.constructor); // logs Date()
console.log(myRegExp.constructor); // logs RegExp()
console.log(myError.constructor); // logs Error()

</script></body></html>
```

By using the new operator, we are telling the JavaScript interpreter that we would like an object that is an instance of the corresponding constructor function. For example, in the code above, the Date() constructor function is used to create date objects. The Date() constructor function is a cookie cutter for date objects. That is, it produces date objects from a default pattern defined by the Date() constructor function.

At this point, you should be well acquainted with creating object instances from native [e.g., new String('foo')] and user-defined constructor functions [e.g., new Person(true, 33, 'male')].

 Note
Keep in mind that Math is a static object—a container for other methods—and is not a constructor that uses the new operator.

Creating Shorthand/Literal Values from Constructors

JavaScript provides shortcuts—called "literals"—for manufacturing most of the native object values without having to use new Foo() or new Bar(). For the most part, the literal syntax accomplishes the same thing as using the new operator. The exceptions are: Number(), String(), and Boolean()—see notes below.

If you come from other programming backgrounds, you are likely more familiar with the literal way of creating objects. Below, I instantiate the native JavaScript constructors using the new operator and then create corresponding literal equivalents.

Live Code (*http://jsfiddle.net/javascriptenlightenment/Nbkw4/*)

```
<!DOCTYPE html><html lang="en"><body><script>

var myNumber = new Number(23); // an object
var myNumberLiteral = 23; // primitive number value, not an object

var myString = new String('male'); // an object
var myStringLiteral = 'male'; // primitive string value, not an object

var myBoolean = new Boolean(false); // an object
var myBooleanLiteral = false; // primitive boolean value, not an object

var myObject = new Object();
var myObjectLiteral = {};

var myArray = new Array('foo', 'bar');
var myArrayLiteral = ['foo', 'bar'];

var myFunction = new Function("x", "y", "return x*y");
var myFunctionLiteral = function(x, y) {return x*y};
```

```
var myRegExp = new RegExp('\bt[a-z]+\b');
var myRegExpLiteral = /\bt[a-z]+\b/;

// verify that literals are created from same constructor

console.log(myNumber.constructor,myNumberLiteral.constructor);
console.log(myString.constructor,myStringLiteral.constructor);
console.log(myBoolean.constructor,myBooleanLiteral.constructor);
console.log(myObject.constructor,myObjectLiteral.constructor);
console.log(myArray.constructor,myArrayLiteral.constructor);
console.log(myFunction.constructor,myFunctionLiteral.constructor);
console.log(myRegExp.constructor,myRegExpLiteral.constructor);


</script></body></html>
```

What you need to take away here is the fact that, in general, using literals simply conceals the underlying process identical to using the new operator. Maybe more importantly, it's a lot more convenient!

Okay, things are a little more complicated with respect to the primitive string, number, and boolean values. In these cases, literal values take on the characteristics of primitive values rather than complex object values. See my note below.

Note

When using literal values for string, number, and boolean, an actual complex object is never created until the value is treated as an object. In other words, you are dealing with a primitive datatype until you attempt to use methods or retrieve properties associated with the constructor (e.g., var charactersInFoo = 'foo'.length). When this happens, JavaScript creates a wrapper object for the literal value behind the scenes, allowing the value to be treated as an object. Then, after the method is called, JavaScript discards the wrapper object and the value returns to a literal type. This is why string, number, and boolean are considered primitive (or simple) datatypes. I hope this clarifies the misconception that "everything in JavaScript is an object" with the concept that "everything in JavaScript can act like an object."

Primitive (a.k.a. Simple) Values

The JavaScript values 5, 'foo', true, and false, as well as null and undefined, are considered primitive because they are *irreducible*. That is, a number is a number, a string is a string, a boolean is either true or false, and null and undefined are just that, null and undefined. These values are inherently simple, and do not represent values that can be made up of other values.

Examine the code below and ask yourself if the string, number, boolean, null, and undefined values could be more complex. Contrast this to what you know of an Object() instance or Array() instance or really any complex object.

Live Code (*http://jsfiddle.net/javascriptenlightenment/xUQTC/*)

```
<!DOCTYPE html><html lang="en"><body><script>

var myString = 'string'
var myNumber = 10;
var myBoolean = false; // could be true or false, but that is it
var myNull = null;
var myUndefined = undefined;

console.log(myString, myNumber, myBoolean, myNull, myUndefined);

/* Consider that a complex object like array or object can be made up of multiple
primitive values, and thus becomes a complex set of multiple values. */

var myObject = {
    myString: 'string',
    myNumber: 10,
    myBoolean: false,
    myNull: null,
    myUndefined: undefined
};

console.log(myObject);

var myArray = ['string', 10, false, null, undefined];

console.log(myArray);

</script></body></html>
```

Quite simply, primitive values represent the lowest form (i.e., simplest) of datum/ information available in JavaScript.

 Notes

- As opposed to creating values with literal syntax, when a String(), Number(), or Boolean() value is created using the new keyword, the object created is actually a complex object.

- It's critical that you understand the fact that the String(), Number(), and Boolean() constructors are dual-purpose constructors used to create literal/primitive values as well as complex values. These constructors do not always return objects, but instead, when used without the new operator, can return a primitive representation of the actual complex object value.

The Primitive Values null, undefined, "string", 10, true, and false Are Not Objects

The null and undefined values are such trivial values that they do not require a constructor function, nor the use of the new operator to establish them as a JavaScript value. To use null or undefined, all you do is use them as if they were an operator. The remaining primitive values string, number, and boolean, while technically returned from a constructor function, are not objects.

Below, I contrast the difference between primitive values and the rest of the native Java-Script objects.

Live Code (*http://jsfiddle.net/javascriptenlightenment/ZwgqD/*)

```
<!DOCTYPE html><html lang="en"><body><script>

/* no object is created when producing primitive values,
notice no use of the "new" keyword */
var primitiveString1 = "foo";
var primitiveString2 = String('foo');
var primitiveNumber1 = 10;
var primitiveNumber2 = Number('10');
var primitiveBoolean1 = true;
var primitiveBoolean2 = Boolean('true');

// confirm the typeof is not object
console.log(typeof primitiveString1, typeof primitiveString2);
  // logs 'string,string'
console.log(typeof primitiveNumber1, typeof primitiveNumber2);
  // logs 'number,number,
console.log(typeof primitiveBoolean1, typeof primitiveBoolean2);
  // logs 'boolean,boolean'

// versus the usage of a constructor and new keyword for creating objects

var myNumber = new Number(23);
var myString = new String('male');
var myBoolean = new Boolean(false);
var myObject = new Object();
var myArray = new Array('foo', 'bar');
var myFunction = new Function("x", "y", "return x * y");
var myDate = new Date();
var myRegExp = new RegExp('\\bt[a-z]+\\b');
var myError = new Error('Crap!');

// logs 'object object object object object function object function object'
console.log(
typeof myNumber,
typeof myString,
typeof myBoolean,
```

```
typeof myObject,
typeof myArray,
typeof myFunction, // BE AWARE typeof returns function for all function objects
typeof myDate,
typeof myRegExp, // BE AWARE typeof returns function for RegExp()
typeof myError
);

</script></body></html>
```

What I would like you to grasp from the previous code example is that primitive values are not objects. Primitive values are special in that they are used to represent simple values.

How Primitive Values Are Stored/Copied in JavaScript

It is extremely important to grok that primitive values are stored and manipulated at "face value." It might sound simple, but this means that if I store the string value `"foo"` in a variable called `myString`, then the value `"foo"` is literally stored in memory as such. Why is this important? Once you begin manipulating (e.g., copying) values, you have to be equipped with this knowledge, because primitive values are copied literally.

In the example below, we store a copy of the `myString` value (`'foo'`) in the variable `myStringCopy`, and its value is literally copied. Even if we change the original value, the copied value, referenced by the variable `myStringCopy`, remains unchanged.

Live Code (*http://jsfiddle.net/javascriptenlightenment/Gh3dW/*)

```
<!DOCTYPE html><html lang="en"><body><script>

var myString = 'foo' // create a primitive string object
var myStringCopy = myString; // copy its value into a new variable

var myString = null; // manipulate the value stored in the myString variable

/* The original value from myString was copied to myStringCopy. This is confirmed
by updating the value of myString then checking the value of myStringCopy */

console.log(myString, myStringCopy); // logs 'null foo'


</script></body></html>
```

The takeaway here is that primitive values are stored and manipulated as irreducible *values*. Referring to them transfers their value. In the example above, we *copied, or cloned*, the `myString` value to the variable `myStringCopy`. When we updated the `my String` value, the `myStringCopy` value still had a copy of the old `myString` value. Remember this and contrast the mechanics here with complex objects (discussed below).

Primitive Values Are Equal by Value

Primitives can be compared to see if their values are literally the same. As logic would suggest, if you compare a variable containing the numeric value 10 with another variable containing the numeric value 10, JavaScript will consider these equal because 10 is the same as 10 (i.e., 10 === 10). The same, of course, would apply if you compare the primitive string 'foo' to another primitive string with a value of 'foo'. The comparison would say that they are equal to each other based on their value (i.e., 'foo' === 'foo').

In the code below, I demonstrate the "equal by value" concept using primitive numbers, as well as contrast this with a complex number object.

Live Code (*http://jsfiddle.net/javascriptenlightenment/NewQU/*)

```
<!DOCTYPE html><html lang="en"><body><script>

var price1 = 10;
var price2 = 10;
var price3 = new Number('10'); // a complex numeric object because new was used
var price4 = price3;

console.log(price1 === price2); // logs true

/* logs false because price3 contains a complex number object and price 1 is
a primitive value */
console.log(price1 === price3);

// logs true because complex values are equal by reference, not value
console.log(price4 === price3);

// what if we update the price4 variable to contain a primitive value?
price4 = 10;

console.log(price4 === price3); /* logs false: price4 is now primitive
                                    rather than complex */

</script></body></html>
```

The takeaway here is that primitives, when compared, will check to see if the expressed *values* are equal. When a string, number, or boolean value is created using the new keyword [e.g., new Number('10')], the value is no longer primitive. As such, comparison does not work the same as if the value had been created via literal syntax. This is not surprising, given that primitive values are stored by value (does 10 === 10?), while complex values are stored by reference (do price3 and price4 contain a reference to the same value?).

The String, Number, and Boolean Primitive Values Act Like Objects When Used Like Objects

When a primitive value is used as if it were an object created by a constructor, JavaScript converts it to an object in order to respond to the expression at hand, but then discards the object qualities and changes it back to a primitive value. In the code below, I take primitive values and showcase what happens when the values are treated like objects.

Live Code (*http://jsfiddle.net/javascriptenlightenment/gSTNp/*)

```
<!DOCTYPE html><html lang="en"><body><script>

// Produce primitive values
var myNull = null;
var myUndefined = undefined;
var primitiveString1 = "foo";
var primitiveString2 = String('foo'); // did not use new, so we get primitive
var primitiveNumber1 = 10;
var primitiveNumber2 = Number('10'); // did not use new, so we get primitive
var primitiveBoolean1 = true;
var primitiveBoolean2 = Boolean('true'); // did not use new, so we get primitive

/* Access the toString() property method (inherited by objects from
object.prototype) to demonstrate that the primitive values are converted to
objects when treated like objects. */

// logs "string string"
console.log(primitiveString1.toString(), primitiveString2.toString());

// logs "number number"
console.log(primitiveNumber1.toString(), primitiveNumber2.toString());

// logs "boolean boolean"
console.log(primitiveBoolean1.toString(), primitiveBoolean2.toString());

/* This will throw an error and not show up in firebug lite, as null and
undefined do not convert to objects and do not have constructors. */
console.log(myNull.toString());
console.log(myUndefined.toString());

</script></body></html>
```

In the above code example, all of the primitive values (except null and undefined) are converted to objects, so as to leverage the toString() method, and then are returned to primitive values once the method is invoked and returned.

Complex (a.k.a. Composite) Values

The native object constructors `Object()`, `Array()`, `Function()`, `Date()`, `Error()`, and `RegExp()` are complex because they can contain one or or more primitive or complex values. Essentially, complex values can be made up of many different types of JavaScript objects. It could be said that complex objects have an unknown size in memory because complex objects can contain any value and not a specific known value. In the code below, we create an object and an array that houses all of the primitive objects.

Live Code (http://jsfiddle.net/javascriptenlightenment/JeFqt/)

```
<!DOCTYPE html><html lang="en"><body><script>

var object = {
    myString: 'string',
    myNumber: 10,
    myBoolean: false,
    myNull: null,
    myUndefined: undefined
};

var array = ['string', 10, false, null, undefined];

/* Contrast this to the simplicity of the primitive values below. In a primitive
form, none of the values below can be more complex than what you see while
complex values can encapsulate any of the JavaScript values (seen above). */

var myString = 'string';
var myNumber = 10;
var myBoolean = false;
var myNull = null;
var myUndefined = undefined;

</script></body></html>
```

The takeaway here is that complex values are a composite of values and differ in complexity and composition to primitive values.

Note
The term "complex object" has also been expressed in other writings as "composite objects" or "reference types." If it's not obvious, all these names describe the nature of a JavaScript value excluding primitive values. Primitive values are not "referenced by value" and cannot represent a composite (i.e., a thing made up of several parts or elements) of other values. Complex objects, on the other hand, are "referenced by value" and can contain or encapsulate other values.

How Complex Values Are Stored/Copied in JavaScript

It is extremely important to grok that complex values are stored and manipulated by *reference*. When creating a variable containing a complex object, the value is stored in memory at an address. When you reference a complex object, you're using its name (i.e., variable or object property) to retrieve the value at that address in memory. The implications are significant when you consider what happens when you attempt to copy a complex value. Below, we create an object stored in the variable myObject. Then the value in myObject is copied to the variable copyOfMyObject. Really, it is not a copy of the object—more like a copy of the address of the object.

Live Code (*http://jsfiddle.net/javascriptenlightenment/hypZC/*)

```
<!DOCTYPE html><html lang="en"><body><script>

var myObject = {};

var copyOfMyObject = myObject; /* not copied by value,
                                  just the reference is copied */

myObject.foo = 'bar'; // manipulate the value stored in myObject

/* Now if we log myObject and copyOfMyObject, they will have a foo property
because they reference the same object. */
console.log(myObject, copyOfMyObject); /* logs 'Object { foo="bar"}
                                          Object { foo="bar"}' */

</script></body></html>
```

What you need to realize is that, unlike primitive values that would copy a value, objects (a.k.a. complex values) are stored by reference. As such, the reference (a.k.a. address) is copied, but not the actual value. This means that objects are not copied at all. Like I said, what is copied is the address or reference to the object in the memory stack. In our code example, myObject and copyOfMyObject point to the same object stored in memory.

The big takeaway here is that when you change a complex value—because it is stored by reference—you change the value stored in all variables that reference that complex value. In our code example, both myObject and copyOfMyObject are changed when you update the object stored in either variable.

Notes

- When the values String(), Number(), and Boolean() are created using the new keyword, or converted to complex objects behind the scenes, the values continue to be stored/copied by value. So, even though primitive values can be treated like complex values, they do not take on the quality of being copied by reference.

- To truly make a copy of an object, you have to extract the values from the old object, and inject them into a new object.

Complex Objects Are Equal by Reference

When comparing complex objects, they are equal only when they reference the same object (i.e., have the same address). Two variables containing identical objects are not equal to each other since they do not actually point at the same object.

Below, objectFoo and objectBar have the same properties and are, in fact, identical objects, but when asked if they are equal via ===, JavaScript tells us they are not.

Live Code (*http://jsfiddle.net/javascriptenlightenment/g4CfS/*)

```
<!DOCTYPE html><html lang="en"><body><script>

var objectFoo = {same: 'same'};
var objectBar = {same: 'same'};

/* logs false, JS does not care that they are identical
and of the same object type */
console.log(objectFoo === objectBar);

// how complex objects are measured for equality
var objectA = {foo: 'bar'};
var objectB = objectA;

console.log(objectA === objectB); /* logs true because they reference
                                     the same object */

</script></body></html>
```

The takeaway here is that variables that point to a complex object in memory are equal only because they are using the same "address." Conversely, two independently created objects are not equal even if they are of the same type and possess the exact same properties.

Complex Objects Have Dynamic Properties

A new variable that points to an existing complex object does not copy the object. This is why complex objects are sometimes called reference objects. A complex object can have as many references as you want, and they will always refer to the same object, even as that object changes.

Live Code (*http://jsfiddle.net/javascriptenlightenment/SSsVC/*)

```
<!DOCTYPE html><html lang="en"><body><script>

var objA = {property: 'value'};
var pointer1 = objA;
var pointer2 = pointer1;

// update the objA.property, and all references (pointer1 and pointer2) are updated
objA.property = null;

/* logs 'null null null' because objA, pointer1, and pointer2 all reference
the same object */
console.log(objA.property, pointer1.property, pointer2.property);

</script></body></html>
```

This allows for dynamic object properties because you can define an object, create references, update the object, and all of the variables referring to the object will "get" that update.

The typeof Operator Used on Primitive and Complex Values

The typeof operator can be used to return the type of value you are dealing with. But the values returned from it are not exactly consistent or what some might say, logical. The following code exhibits the returned values from using the typeof operator.

Live Code (*http://jsfiddle.net/javascriptenlightenment/QM95R/*)

```
<!DOCTYPE html><html lang="en"><body><script>

// primitive values
var myNull = null;
var myUndefined = undefined;
var primitiveString1 = "string";
var primitiveString2 = String('string');
var primitiveNumber1 = 10;
var primitiveNumber2 = Number('10');
var primitiveBoolean1 = true;
var primitiveBoolean2 = Boolean('true');
```

```
console.log(typeof myNull); // logs object? WHAT? Be aware...
console.log(typeof myUndefined); // logs undefined
console.log(typeof primitiveString1, typeof primitiveString2);
   // logs string string
console.log(typeof primitiveNumber1, typeof primitiveNumber2);
   // logs number number
console.log(typeof primitiveBoolean1, typeof primitiveBoolean2);
   // logs boolean boolean

// Complex Values
var myNumber = new Number(23);
var myString = new String('male');
var myBoolean = new Boolean(false);
var myObject = new Object();
var myArray = new Array('foo', 'bar');
var myFunction = new Function("x", "y", "return x * y");
var myDate = new Date();
var myRegExp = new RegExp('\\bt[a-z]+\\b');
var myError = new Error('Crap!');

console.log(typeof myNumber); // logs object
console.log(typeof myString); // logs object
console.log(typeof myBoolean); // logs object
console.log(typeof myObject); // logs object
console.log(typeof myArray); // logs object
console.log(typeof myFunction); // logs function? WHAT? Be aware...
console.log(typeof myDate); // logs object
console.log(typeof myRegExp); // logs function? WHAT? Be aware...
console.log(typeof myError); // logs object

</script></body></html>
```

When using this operator on values, you should be aware of the potential values returned given the type of value (primitive or complex) that you are dealing with.

Dynamic Properties Allow for Mutable Objects

Complex objects are made up of dynamic properties. This allows for user-defined objects—and most of the native objects—to be mutated. This means that the majority of objects in JavaScript can be updated or changed at any time. Because of this, we can change the native pre-configured nature of JavaScript itself by augmenting its native objects. However, I am not telling you to do this; in fact, I do not think you should. But let's not cloud what is possible with opinions.

This means it's possible to store properties on native constructors and add new methods to the native objects with additions to their prototype objects.

In the code below, I mutate the String() constructor function and String.prototype.

Live Code (*http://jsfiddle.net/javascriptenlightenment/QvbDw/*)

```
<!DOCTYPE html><html lang="en"><body><script>

/* augment the built-in String constructor Function() with the augmentedProperties
property */
String.augmentedProperties = [];

if (!String.prototype.trimIT) { // if the prototype does not have trimIT() add it
    String.prototype.trimIT = function() {
        return this.replace(/^\s+|\s+$/g, '');
    }

    // now add trimIT string to the augmentedProperties array
    String.augmentedProperties.push('trimIT');
}
var myString = '  trim me  ';
console.log(myString.trimIT()); /* invoke our custom trimIT string method,
                                   logs 'trim me' */

console.log(String.augmentedProperties.join()); // logs 'trimIT'

</script></body></html>
```

I want to drive home the fact that objects in JavaScript are dynamic. This allows objects in JavaScript to be mutated. Essentially, the entire language can be mutated into a custom version (e.g., `trimIT` string method). Again, I am not recommending this—I am just pointing out that it is part of the nature of objects in JavaScript.

 Note
Careful! If you mutate the native inner workings of JavaScript, you potentially have a custom version of JavaScript to deal with. Proceed with caution, as most people will assume that JavaScript is the same whenever it's available.

All Constructor Instances Have Constructor Properties that Point to Their Constructor Function

When any object is instantiated, the `constructor` property is created behind the scenes as a property of that object/instance. This points to the constructor function that created the object. Below, we create an `Object()` object, stored in the `foo` variable, and then verify that the `constructor` property is available for the object we created.

Live Code (*http://jsfiddle.net/javascriptenlightenment/ZtewV/*)

```
<!DOCTYPE html><html lang="en"><body><script>
```

```
var foo = {};

console.log(foo.constructor === Object) /* logs true, because object()
                                  constructed foo */
console.log(foo.constructor) // points to the Object() constructor function

</script></body></html>
```

This can be handy: if I'm working with some instance, and I can't see who or what created it (especially if it was someone else's code), I can determine if it's an array, an object, or whatever.

Below, you can see that I have instantiated most of the pre-configured objects that come included with the JavaScript language. Note that using the constructor property on literal/primitive values correctly resolves (i.e., points) to the right constructor.

Live Code (*http://jsfiddle.net/javascriptenlightenment/yJqaF/*)

```
<!DOCTYPE html><html lang="en"><body><script>

var myNumber = new Number('23');
var myNumberL = 23; // literal shorthand
var myString = new String('male');
var myStringL = 'male'; // literal shorthand
var myBoolean = new Boolean('true');
var myBooleanL = true; // literal shorthand
var myObject = new Object();
var myObjectL = {}; // literal shorthand
var myArray = new Array();
var myArrayL = []; // literal shorthand
var myFunction = new Function();
var myFunctionL = function() {}; // literal shorthand
var myDate = new Date();
var myRegExp = new RegExp('/./');
var myRegExpL = /./; // literal shorthand
var myError = new Error();

console.log( // all of these return true
    myNumber.constructor === Number,
    myNumberL.constructor === Number,
    myString.constructor === String,
    myStringL.constructor === String,
    myBoolean.constructor === Boolean,
    myBooleanL.constructor === Boolean,
    myObject.constructor === Object,
    myObjectL.constructor === Object,
    myArray.constructor === Array,
    myArrayL.constructor === Array,
    myFunction.constructor === Function,
    myFunctionL.constructor === Function,
    myDate.constructor === Date,
    myRegExp.constructor === RegExp,
```

```
    myRegExpL.constructor === RegExp,
    myError.constructor === Error
);

</script></body></html>
```

The constructor property also works on user-defined constructor functions. Below, we define a `CustomConstructor()` constructor function, then using the keyword `new`, we invoke the function to produce an object. Once we have our object, we can then leverage the constructor property.

Live Code (*http://jsfiddle.net/javascriptenlightenment/MDs2t/*)

```
<!DOCTYPE html><html lang="en"><body><script>

var CustomConstructor = function CustomConstructor(){ return 'Wow!'; };
var instanceOfCustomObject = new CustomConstructor();

// logs true
console.log(instanceOfCustomObject.constructor === CustomConstructor);

// returns a reference to CustomConstructor() function
// returns 'function() { return 'Wow!'; };'
console.log(instanceOfCustomObject.constructor);

</script></body></html>
```

 Notes

- You might be confused as to why primitive values have constructor properties that point to constructor functions when objects are not returned. By using a primitive value, the constructor is still called, so there is still a relationship with primitive values and constructor functions. However, the end result is a primitive value.

- If you would like the constructor property to log the actual name of the constructor for user-defined constructor function expressions, you have to give the constructor function expressions an actual name (e.g., `var Person = function Person(){};`).

Verify that an Object Is an Instance of a Particular Constructor Function

By using the `instanceof` operator, we can determine (true or false) if an object is an instance of a particular constructor function.

Below, we are verifying if the object `InstanceOfCustomObject` is an instance of the `CustomConstructor` constructor function. This works with user-defined objects as well as native objects created with the new operator.

Live Code (*http://jsfiddle.net/javascriptenlightenment/g9Tt6/*)

```
<!DOCTYPE html><html lang="en"><body><script>

// user-defined object constructor
var CustomConstructor = function() {this.foo = 'bar';};

// instantiate an instance of CustomConstructor
var instanceOfCustomObject = new CustomConstructor();

console.log(instanceOfCustomObject instanceof CustomConstructor); // logs true

// works the same as a native object
console.log(new Array('foo') instanceof Array) // logs true

</script></body></html>
```

Notes

- One thing to watch out for when dealing with the `instanceof` operator is that it will return true any time you ask if an object is an instance of Object since all objects inherit from the `Object()` Constructor.

- The `instanceof` operator will return false when dealing with primitive values that leverage object wrappers (e.g., `'foo' instanceof String` // returns false). Had the string `'foo'` been created with the new operator, the `instanceof` operator would have returned true. So, keep in mind that `instanceof` really only works with complex objects and instances created from constructor functions that return objects.

An Instance Created From a Constructor Can Have Its Own Independent Properties (Instance Properties)

In JavaScript, objects can be augmented at any time (i.e., dynamic properties). As previously mentioned, and to be exact, JavaScript has *mutable objects*. This means that objects created from a constructor function can be augmented with properties.

Below, I create an instance from the `Array()` constructor and then augment it with its own property.

Live Code (*http://jsfiddle.net/javascriptenlightenment/RuQfJ/*)

```
<!DOCTYPE html><html lang="en"><body><script>

var myArray = new Array();
myArray.prop = 'test';

console.log(myArray.prop) // logs 'test'

</script></body></html>
```

This could be done with `Object()`, `RegExp()`, or any of the other non-primitive constructors—even `Boolean()`.

Live Code (*http://jsfiddle.net/javascriptenlightenment/GnbPf/*)

```
<!DOCTYPE html><html lang="en"><body><script>

/* this can be done with any of the native constructors that actually
produce an object */
var myString = new String();
var myNumber = new Number();
var myBoolean = new Boolean(true);
var myObject = new Object();
var myArray = new Array();
var myFunction = new Function('return 2+2');
var myRegExp = new RegExp('\bt[a-z]+\b');

myString.prop = 'test';
myNumber.prop = 'test';
myBoolean.prop = 'test';
myObject.prop = 'test';
myArray.prop = 'test';
myFunction.prop = 'test';
myRegExp.prop = 'test';

// logs 'test', 'test', 'test', 'test', 'test', 'test', 'test'
console.log(myString.prop,myNumber.prop,myBoolean.prop,myObject.prop,
  myArray.prop,myFunction.prop, myRegExp.prop);

// be aware: instance properties do not work with primitive/literal values
var myString = 'string';
var myNumber = 1;
var myBoolean = true;

myString.prop = true;
myNumber.prop = true;
myBoolean.prop = true;

// logs undefined, undefined, undefined
console.log(myString.prop, myNumber.prop, myBoolean.prop);

</script></body></html>
```

Adding properties to objects created from a constructor function is not uncommon. Remember: object instances created from constructor functions are just plain old objects.

Note
Keep in mind that, besides their own properties, instances can have properties inherited from the prototype chain. Or, as we just saw in the code, properties added to the constructor after instantiation. This highlights the dynamic nature of objects in JavaScript.

The Semantics of "JavaScript Objects" and "Object() Objects"

Do not confuse the general term "JavaScript objects", which refers to the notion of objects in JavaScript, with `Object()` objects. An `Object()` object [e.g., `var myObject = new Object()`] is a very specific type of value expressed in JavaScript. Just as an `Array()` object is a type of object called *array*, an `Object()` object is a type of object called *object*. The gist is that the `Object()` constructor function produces an empty generic object container, which is referred to as an `Object()` object. Similarly, the `Array()` constructor function produces an array object, and we refer to these objects as `Array()` objects.

In this book, the term "JavaScript object" is used to refer to all objects in JavaScript, because most of the values in JavaScript can act like objects. This is due to the fact that the majority of JavaScript values are created from a native constructor function which produces a very specific type of object.

What you need to remember is that an `Object()` object is a very specific kind of value. It's a generic empty object. Do not confuse this with the term "JavaScript objects" used to refer to most of the values that can be expressed in JavaScript as an object.

CHAPTER 2

Working with Objects and Properties

Complex Objects Can Contain Most of the JavaScript Values as Properties

A complex object can hold any permitted JavaScript value. Below, I create an Object() object called myObject and then add properties representing the majority of values available in JavaScript.

Live Code (*http://jsfiddle.net/javascriptenlightenment/JAEMd/*)

```
<!DOCTYPE html><html lang="en"><body><script>

var myObject = {};

/* contain properties inside of myObject representing most of the native
JavaScript values */

myObject.myFunction = function() {};
myObject.myArray = [];
myObject.myString = 'string';
myObject.myNumber = 33;
myObject.myDate = new Date();
myObject.myRegExp = /a/;
myObject.myNull = null;
myObject.myUndefined = undefined;
myObject.myObject = {};
myObject.myMath_PI = Math.PI;
myObject.myError = new Error('Crap!');

console.log(myObject.myFunction,myObject.myArray,myObject.myString,
   myObject.myNumber,myObject.myDate,myObject.myRegExp,myObject.myNull,
   myObject.myNull,myObject.myUndefined,myObject.myObject,
   myObject.myMath_PI,myObject.myError);
```

```
/* works the same with any of the complex objects, for example a function */

var myFunction = function() {};

myFunction.myFunction = function() {};
myFunction.myArray = [];
myFunction.myString = 'string';
myFunction.myNumber = 33;
myFunction.myDate = new Date();
myFunction.myRegExp = /a/;
myFunction.myNull = null;
myFunction.myUndefined = undefined;
myFunction.myObject = {};
myFunction.myMath_PI = Math.PI;
myFunction.myError = new Error('Crap!');

console.log(myFunction.myFunction,myFunction.myArray,myFunction.myString,
    myFunction.myNumber,myFunction.myDate,myFunction.myRegExp,myFunction.myNull,
    myFunction.myNull,myFunction.myUndefined,myFunction.myObject,
    myFunction.myMath_PI,myFunction.myError);

</script></body></html>
```

The simple takeaway here is that complex objects can contain—or refer to—anything you can nominally express in JavaScript. You should not be surprised when you see this done, as all of the native objects can be mutated. This even applies to String(), Number(), and Boolean() values in their object form—i.e., when they are created with the new operator.

Encapsulating Complex Objects in a Programmatically Beneficial Way

The Object(), Array(), and Function() objects can contain other complex objects. Below, I demonstrate this by setting up an object tree using Object() objects.

Live Code (*http://jsfiddle.net/javascriptenlightenment/mLYfe/*)

```
<!DOCTYPE html><html lang="en"><body><script>

// encapsulation using objects, creates object chains
var object1 = {
    object1_1: {
        object1_1_1: {foo: 'bar'},
        object1_1_2: {},
    },
    object1_2: {
        object1_2_1: {},
        object1_2_2: {},
    }
};
```

```
console.log(object1.object1_1.object1_1_1.foo); // logs 'bar'

</script></body></html>
```

The same thing could be done with an `Array()` object (a.k.a. multidimensional array), or with a `Function()` object.

Live Code (*http://jsfiddle.net/javascriptenlightenment/9J6Ya/*)

```
<!DOCTYPE html><html lang="en"><body><script>

// encapsulation using arrays, creates multidimensional array chain
var myArray= [[[]]]; /* an empty array, inside an empty array,
                        inside an empty array */

/* Here is an example of encapsulation using functions: an empty function
inside an empty function inside an empty function. */
var myFunction = function() {
   // empty
   var myFunction = function() {
       // empty
       var myFunction = function() {
          // empty
       };
   };
};

// we can get crazy and mix and match too
var foo = [{foo: [{bar: {say: function() {return 'hi';}}}]}];
console.log(foo[0].foo[0].bar.say()); // logs 'hi'

</script></body></html>
```

The main takeaway here is that some of the complex objects are designed to encapsulate other objects in a programmatically beneficial way.

Getting/Setting/Updating an Object's Properties Using Dot Notation or Bracket Notation

We can get, set, or update an object's properties using either *dot notation* or *bracket notation*.

Below, I demonstrate dot notation, which is accomplished by using the object name followed by a period and then followed by the property to get, set, or update (e.g., *objectName.property*).

Live Code (*http://jsfiddle.net/javascriptenlightenment/DYkey/*)

```
<!DOCTYPE html><html lang="en"><body><script>
```

```
// create cody Object() object
var cody = new Object();

// setting properties
cody.living = true;
cody.age = 33;
cody.gender = 'male';
cody.getGender = function() {return cody.gender;};

// getting properties
console.log(
    cody.living,
    cody.age,
    cody.gender,
    cody.getGender()
); // logs 'true 33 male male'

// updating properties, exactly like setting
cody.living = false;
cody.age = 99;
cody.gender = 'female';
cody.getGender = function() {return 'Gender = ' + cody.gender;};

console.log(cody);

</script></body></html>
```

Dot notation is the most common notation for getting, setting, or updating an object's properties.

Bracket notation, unless required, is not as commonly used. Below, I replace the dot notation used above with bracket notation. The object name is followed by an opening bracket, the property name (in quotes), and then a closing bracket:

Live Code (*http://jsfiddle.net/javascriptenlightenment/94GXg/*)

```
<!DOCTYPE html><html lang="en"><body><script>

// creating cody Object() object
var cody = new Object();

// setting properties
cody['living'] = true;
cody['age'] = 33;
cody['gender'] = 'male';
cody['getGender'] = function() {return cody.gender;};

// getting properties
console.log(
    cody['living'],
    cody['age'],
    cody['gender'],
```

```
    cody['getGender']() // just slap the function invocation on the end!
); // logs 'true 33 male male'

// updating properties, very similar to setting
cody['living'] = false;
cody['age'] = 99;
cody['gender'] = 'female';
cody['getGender'] = function() {return 'Gender = ' + cody.gender;};

console.log(cody);

</script></body></html>
```

Bracket notation can be very handy when you need to access a property key and what you have to work with is a variable that contains a string value representing the property name. Below, I demonstrate the advantage of bracket notation over dot notation by using it to access the property foobar. I do this using two variables that, when joined, produce the string version of the property key contained in foobarObject.

Live Code (*http://jsfiddle.net/javascriptenlightenment/RQB6N/*)

```
<!DOCTYPE html><html lang="en"><body><script>

var foobarObject = {foobar: 'Foobar is code for no code'};

var string1 = 'foo';
var string2 = 'bar';

console.log(foobarObject[string1 + string2]); // Let's see dot notation do this!

</script></body></html>
```

Additionally, bracket notation can come in handy for getting at property names that are invalid JavaScript identifiers. Below, I use a number and a reserved keyword as a property name (valid as a string) that only bracket notation can access.

Live Code (*http://jsfiddle.net/javascriptenlightenment/D6GhN/*)

```
<!DOCTYPE html><html lang="en"><body><script>

var myObject = {'123':'zero','class':'foo'};

// Let's see dot notation do this! Keep in mind 'class' is a keyword in JavaScript
console.log(myObject['123'], myObject['class']); // logs 'zero foo'

// it can't do what bracket notation can do, in fact it causes an error
// console.log(myObject.0, myObject.class);

</script></body></html>
```

Notes

- Because objects can contain other objects, it is not uncommon to see `cody.object.object.object.object` or `cody['object']['object']['object']['object']`. This is called object chaining. The encapsulation of object(s) can go on indefinitely.

- Objects are mutable in JavaScript, meaning that getting, setting, or updating them can be performed on most objects at any time. By using the bracket notation (e.g., `cody['age']`), you can mimic Associative Arrays found in other languages.

- If a property inside an object is a method, all you have to do is use the `()` operators [e.g., `cody.getGender()`] to invoke the property method.

Deleting Object Properties

The `delete` operator can be used to completely remove properties from an object. Below, we delete the `bar` property from the `foo` object.

Live Code (*http://jsfiddle.net/javascriptenlightenment/Zwg8T/*)

```
<!DOCTYPE html><html lang="en"><body><script>

var foo = {bar: 'bar'};
delete foo.bar;
console.log('bar' in foo); // logs false, because bar was deleted from foo

</script></body></html>
```

Notes

- Delete will not delete properties that are found on the prototype chain.

- Deleting is the only way to actually remove a property from an object. Setting the property to `undefined` or `null` only changes the value of a property. It does not remove the property from the object.

How References to Object Properties Are Resolved

If you attempt to access a property that is not contained in an object, JavaScript will always attempt to find the property or method using the prototype chain. Below, I create an array and then attempt to access a property called `foo` that has not yet been defined.

You might think that because `myArray.foo` is not a property of the `myArray` object, JavaScript will immediately return `undefined`. But JavaScript will look in two more places (`Array.prototype` and then `Object.prototype`) for the value of `foo` before it returns `undefined`.

Live Code (*http://jsfiddle.net/javascriptenlightenment/DjC6E/*)

```
<!DOCTYPE html><html lang="en"><body><script>

var myArray = [];

console.log(myArray.foo); // logs undefined

/* JS will look at Array.prototype for Array.prototype.foo, but it is not there.
Then it will look for it at Object.prototype, but it is not there either,
so undefined is returned! */

</script></body></html>
```

When I attempt to access a property of an object, it will check that object instance for the property. If it has the property, it will return the value of the property, and there is no inheritance occurring because the prototype chain is not leveraged. If the instance does not have the property, JavaScript will then look for it on the object's constructor function `prototype` object.

All object instances have a property that is a secret link [a.k.a. __proto__ (*http://mzl.la/12dULO9*)] to the constructor function that created the instance. This secret link can be leveraged to grab the constructor function, specifically the `prototype` property of the instance's constructor function.

This is one of the most confusing aspects of objects in JavaScript. But let's reason this out. Remember that a function is also an object with properties. It makes sense to allow objects to *inherit* properties from other objects. Just like saying: "Hey *object B*, I would like you to share all the properties that *object A* has." JavaScript wires this all up for native objects by default via the `prototype` object. When you create your own constructor functions, you can leverage prototype chaining as well.

How exactly JavaScript accomplishes this is confusing until you see it for what it is: just a set of rules. Let's create an array to examine the `prototype` property closer.

Live Code (*http://jsfiddle.net/javascriptenlightenment/VBRyb/*)

```
<!DOCTYPE html><html lang="en"><body><script>

// myArray is an Array object
var myArray = ['foo', 'bar'];

console.log(myArray.join()); // join() is actually defined at Array.prototype.join

</script></body></html>
```

Our `Array()` instance is an object with properties and methods. As we access one of the array methods, like `join()`, let's ask ourselves: Does the `myArray` instance created from the `Array()` constructor have its own `join()` method? Let's check.

Live Code (*http://jsfiddle.net/javascriptenlightenment/bceyR/*)

```
<!DOCTYPE html><html lang="en"><body><script>

var myArray = ['foo', 'bar'];

console.log(myArray.hasOwnProperty('join')); // logs false

</script></body></html>
```

No, it does not. Yet `myArray` has access to the `join()` method as if it were its own property. What happened here? Well, you just observed the prototype chain in action. We accessed a property that, although not contained in the `myArray` object, could be found by Java-Script somewhere else. That somewhere else is very specific. When the `Array()` constructor was created by JavaScript, the `join()` method was added (among others) as a property of the `prototype` property of `Array()`.

To reiterate, if you try to access a property on an object that does not contain it, JavaScript will search the `prototype` chain for this value. First it will look at the constructor function that created the object (e.g., `Array`), and inspect its prototype (e.g., `Array.proto type`) to see if the property can be found there. If the first prototype object does not have the property, then JavaScript keeps searching up the chain at the constructor behind the initial constructor. It can do this all the way up to the end of the chain.

Where does the chain end? Let's examine the example again, invoking the `toLocale String()` method on `myArray`.

Live Code (*http://jsfiddle.net/javascriptenlightenment/vVVeM/*)

```
<!DOCTYPE html><html lang="en"><body><script>

// myArray and Array.prototype contains no toLocaleString() method
var myArray = ['foo', 'bar'];

// toLocaleString() is actually defined at Object.prototype.toLocaleString
console.log(myArray.toLocaleString()); // logs 'foo,bar'

</script></body></html>
```

The `toLocaleString()` method is not defined within the `myArray` object. So, the pro-totype chaining rule is invoked and JavaScript looks for the property in the `Array` constructor's `prototype` property (e.g., `Array.prototype`). It is not there either, so the chain rule is invoked again and we look for the property in the `Object()` prototype property (`Object.prototype`). And yes, it is found there. Had it not been found there, JavaScript would have produced an error stating that the property was `undefined`.

Since all `prototype` properties are objects, the final link in the chain is `Object.proto` `type`. There is no other constructor `prototype` property that can be examined.

There is an entire chapter ahead that breaks down the prototype chain into smaller parts, so if this was completely lost on you, read Chapter 8 and then come back to this explanation to solidify your understanding. From this short read on the matter, I hope you understand that when a property is not found (and deemed `undefined`), JavaScript will have looked at several prototype objects to determine that a property is `undefined`. A lookup always occurs, and this lookup process is how JavaScript handles inheritance as well as simple property lookups.

Using hasOwnProperty, Verify That an Object Property Is Not From the Prototype Chain

While the `in` operator can check for properties of an object, including properties from the prototype chain, the `hasOwnProperty` method can check an object for a property that is not from the prototype chain.

Below, we want to know if `myObject` contains the property `foo`, and that it is not inheriting the property from the prototype chain. To do this, we ask if `myObject` has its own property called `foo`.

Live Code (*http://jsfiddle.net/javascriptenlightenment/5ecJb/*)

```
<!DOCTYPE html><html lang="en"><body><script>

var myObject = {foo: 'value'};

console.log(myObject.hasOwnProperty('foo')) // logs true

// vs. a property from the prototype chain
console.log(myObject.hasOwnProperty('toString'); // logs false

</script></body></html>
```

The `hasOwnProperty` method should be leveraged when you need to determine whether a property is local to an object or inherited from the prototype chain.

Checking If an Object Contains a Given Property Using the in Operator

The `in` operator is used to verify (true or false) if an object contains a given property. Below, we are checking to see if `foo` is a property in `myObject`.

Live Code (*http://jsfiddle.net/javascriptenlightenment/z6Bet/*)

```
<!DOCTYPE html><html lang="en"><body><script>

var myObject = {foo: 'value'};
console.log('foo' in myObject); // logs true

</script></body></html>
```

You should be aware that the `in` operator not only checks for properties contained in the object referenced, but also for any properties that object inherits via the `proto type` chain. Thus, the same property lookup rules apply and the property, if not in the current object, will be searched for on the `prototype` chain.

This means that `myObject` in the above code actually contains a `toString` property method via the `prototype` chain (`Object.prototype.toString`), even if we did not specify one (e.g., `myObject.toString = 'foo'`).

Live Code (*http://jsfiddle.net/javascriptenlightenment/Z3B87/*)

```
<!DOCTYPE html><html lang="en"><body><script>

var myObject = {foo: 'value'};
console.log('toString' in myObject); // logs true

</script></body></html>
```

In the last code example, the `toString` property is not literally inside of the `myObject` object. However, it is inherited from `Object.prototype` and so the `in` operator concludes that `myObject` does in fact have an inherited `toString()` property method.

Enumerate (Loop Over) an Object's Properties using the for in Loop

By using `for in`, we can loop over each property in an object. In the code below, we are using the `for in` loop to retrieve the property names from the `cody` object.

Live Code (*http://jsfiddle.net/javascriptenlightenment/fwr2B/*)

```
<!DOCTYPE html><html lang="en"><body><script>

var cody = {
    age : 23,
    gender : 'male'
};

for (var key in cody) { // key is a variable used to represent each property name
    // avoid properties inherited from the prototype chain
    if(cody.hasOwnProperty(key)) {
        console.log(key);
```

```
        }
    }

</script></body></html>
```

Notes

- The `for in` loop has a drawback. It will not only access the properties of the specific object being looped over, but will also include in the loop any properties inherited (via the prototype chain) by the object. Thus, if this is not the desired result (and most of the time it is not), we have to use a simple `if` statement inside of the loop to make sure we only access the properties contained within the specific object we are looping over. This can be done by using the `hasOwnProperty()` method, inherited by all objects.

- The order in which the properties are accessed in the loop is not always in the order they are defined within the loop. Additionally the order in which you defined properties is not necessarily the order they are accessed.

- Only properties that are enumerable (i.e., available when looping over an object's properties) show up with the `for in` loop. For example, the constructor property will not show up. It is possible to check which properties are enumerable with the `propertyIsE numerable()` method (*http://mzl.la/WHAqLy*).

Host Objects versus Native Objects

You should be aware that the environment (e.g., a web browser) in which JavaScript is executed typically contains what are known as *host objects*. Host objects are not part of the ECMAScript implementation, but are available as objects during execution. Of course, the availability and behavior of a host object depends completely on what the host environment provides.

For example, in the web browser environment the window/head object and all of its containing objects (*https://developer.mozilla.org/en/Gecko_DOM_Reference*) [excluding what JavaScript provides] are considered host objects.

Below, I examine the properties of the `window` object.

Live Code (*http://jsfiddle.net/javascriptenlightenment/zn4rY/*)

```
<!DOCTYPE html><html lang="en"><body><script>

for (x in window) {
    console.log(x); //logs all of the properties of the window/head object
}

</script></body></html>
```

You might have noticed that native JavaScript objects are not listed among the host objects. It's fairly common that a browser distinguishes between host objects and native objects.

As it pertains to web browsers, the most famous of all hosted objects is the interface for working with HTML documents, also known as the DOM (*https://developer.mozilla.org/en/DOM/document*). Below, is a method to list all of the objects contained inside the window.document object provided by the browser environment.

Live Code (*http://jsfiddle.net/javascriptenlightenment/fTS7X/*)

```
<!DOCTYPE html><html lang="en"><body><script>

for (x in window.document) {
    console.log();
}

</script></body></html>
```

What I want you to grok here is that the JavaScript specification does not concern itself with host objects and vice versa. There is a dividing line between what JavaScript provides (e.g., JavaScript 1.5, ES3 versus Mozilla's JavaScript 1.6, 1.7, 1.8, 1.8.1, 1.8.5) and what the host environment provides, and these two should not be confused.

Notes

- The host environment (e.g., a web browser) that runs JavaScript code typically provides the *head object* (e.g., window object in a web browser) where the native portions of the language are stored along with host objects (e.g., window.location in a web browser) and user-defined objects (e.g., the code you write to run in a web browser).

- It's not uncommon for a web browser manufacturer as the host of the JavaScript interrupter to push forward the version of JavaScript or add future specifications to JavaScript before they have been approved (e.g., Mozilla's Firefox JavaScript 1.6, 1.8, 1.8.1, 1.8.5).

Enhancing and Extending Objects with Underscore.js

JavaScript 1.5 is lacking when it comes time to seriously manipulate and manage objects. If you are running JavaScript in a web browser, I would like to be bold here and suggest the usage of Underscore.js (*http://documentcloud.github.com/underscore/*) when you need more functionality than is provided by JavaScript 1.5. Underscore.js provides the following functionality when dealing with objects.

These functions work on all objects and arrays:

- `each()`
- `map()`
- `reduce()`
- `reduceRight()`
- `detect()`
- `select()`
- `reject()`
- `all()`
- `any()`
- `include()`
- `invoke()`
- `pluck()`
- `max()`
- `min()`
- `sortBy()`
- `sortIndex()`
- `toArray()`
- `size()`

These functions work on all objects:

- `keys()`
- `values()`
- `functions()`
- `extend()`
- `clone()`

- tap()
- isEqual()
- isEmpty()
- isElement()
- isArray()
- isArguments
- isFunction()
- isString()
- isNumber
- isBoolean
- isDate
- isRegExp
- isNaN
- isNull
- isUndefined

I like this library because it takes advantage of the new native additions to JavaScript where browsers support them, but also provides the same functionality to browsers that do not, all without changing the native implementation of JavaScript unless it has to.

Note

Before you start to use Underscore.js, make sure the functionality you need is not already provided by a JavaScript library or framework that might already be in use in your code.

CHAPTER 3

Object()

Conceptual Overview of Using Object() Objects

Using the built-in `Object()` constructor function, we can create generic empty objects on the fly. In fact, if you remember back to the beginning of Chapter 1, this is exactly what we did by creating the cody object. Let's re-create the cody object.

Live Code (*http://jsfiddle.net/javascriptenlightenment/EZ52Q/*)

```
<!DOCTYPE html><html lang="en"><body><script>

var cody = new Object(); // create an empty object with no properties

for (key in cody) { // confirm that cody is an empty generic object
    if(cody.hasOwnProperty(key)) {
        console.log(key); /* should not see any logs,
                        because cody itself has no properties */
    }
}

</script></body></html>
```

Here, all we are doing is using the `Object()` constructor function to create a generic object called *cody*. You can think of the `Object()` constructor as a cookie cutter for creating empty objects that have no predefined properties or methods (except, of course, those inherited from the prototype chain).

Note

If it's not obvious, the Object() constructor is an object itself. That is, the constructor function is based on an object created from the Function constructor. This can be confusing. Just remember that like the Array constructor, the Object constructor simply spits out blank objects. And yes, you can create all the empty objects you like. However, creating an empty object like *cody* is very different than creating your own constructor function with predefined properties. Make sure you grok that *cody* is just an empty object based on the Object() constructor. To really harness the power of JavaScript, you will need to grok not only how to create empty object containers from Object(), but also how to build your own "class" of objects [e.g., Person()] like the Object() constructor function itself.

Object() Parameters

The Object() constructor function takes one optional parameter. That parameter is the value you would like to create. If you provide no parameter, then a null or undefined value will be assumed.

Live Code (*http://jsfiddle.net/javascriptenlightenment/L5bvU/*)

```
<!DOCTYPE html><html lang="en"><body><script>

// create an empty object with no properties
var cody1 = new Object();
var cody2 = new Object(undefined);
var cody3 = new Object(null);

console.log(typeof cody1, typeof cody2, typeof cody3); /* logs
                                              'object object object' */

</script></body></html>
```

If a value besides null or undefined is passed to the Object() constructor, the value passed will be created as an object. So theoretically, we can use the Object() constructor to create any of the other native objects that have a constructor. Below, I do just that.

Live Code (*http://jsfiddle.net/javascriptenlightenment/M7cgC/*)

```
<!DOCTYPE html><html lang="en"><body><script>

/* Use Object() constructor to create a string, number, array, function, boolean,
and regex object. */

// logs below confirm object creation
console.log(new Object('foo'));
console.log(new Object(1));
```

```
console.log(new Object([]));
console.log(new Object(function() {}));
console.log(new Object(true));
console.log(new Object(/\bt[a-z]+\b/));

/* Creating a string, number, array, function, boolean, and regex object instance
via the Object() constructor is really never done. I am just demonstrating that
it can be done */

</script></body></html>
```

Object() Properties and Methods

The Object() object has the following properties (not including inherited properties and methods):

Properties (e.g., Object.prototype;):

- prototype

Object() Object Instance Properties and Methods

Object() object instances have the following properties and methods:

Instance Properties (e.g., var myObject = {}; myObject.constructor;):

- constructor

Instance Methods (e.g., var myObject = {}; myObject.toString();):

- hasOwnProperty()
- isPrototypeOf()
- propertyIsEnumerable()
- toLocaleString()
- toString()
- valueOf()

Note
The prototype chain ends with Object.prototype and thus all of the properties and methods of Object() (shown above) are inherited by all JavaScript objects.

Creating Object() Objects Using "Object Literals"

Creating an "object literal" entails instantiating an object with or without properties using braces (e.g., var cody = {};). Remember back to the beginning of Chapter 1, when we created the one-off cody object and then gave the cody object properties using dot notation? Let's do that again.

Live Code (*http://jsfiddle.net/javascriptenlightenment/5RBny/*)

```
<!DOCTYPE html><html lang="en"><body><script>

var cody = new Object();
cody.living = true;
cody.age = 33;
cody.gender = 'male';
cody.getGender = function() {return cody.gender;};

console.log(cody); // logs cody object and properties

</script></body></html>
```

Notice in the code above that creating the cody object and its properties took five statements. Using the "object literal" notation, we can express the same cody object in one statement.

Live Code (*http://jsfiddle.net/javascriptenlightenment/aYmTQ/*)

```
<!DOCTYPE html><html lang="en"><body><script>

var cody = {
    living: true,
    age: 23,
    gender: 'male',
    getGender: function() {return cody.gender;}
};
// notice the last property has no comma after it

console.log(cody); // logs cody object and properties

</script>
</body>
```

Using literal notation gives us the ability to create objects, including defined properties, with less code and visually encapsulate the related data. Notice the use of the ; and , operators in a single statement. This is actually the preferred syntax for creating objects in JavaScript because of its terseness and readability.

You should be aware that property names can also be specified as strings:

```
<!DOCTYPE html><html lang="en"><body><script>

var cody = {
    'living': true,
    'age': 23,
    'gender': 'male',
    'getGender': function() {return cody.gender;}
};

console.log(cody); // logs cody object and properties

</script>
</body>
```

It's not necessary to specify properties as strings unless the property name

- is one of the reserved keywords (*https://developer.mozilla.org/en/Core_Java Script_1.5_Reference/Reserved_Words*) [e.g., `class`]
- contains spaces or special characters [anything other than numbers, letters, the dollar sign ($) or the underscore (_) character]
- starts with a number

Note

Careful! The last property of an object should not have a trailing comma. This will cause an error in some JavaScript environments.

All Objects Inherit From Object.prototype

The `Object()` constructor function in JavaScript is special, as its `prototype` property is the last stop in the prototype chain.

Below, I augment the `Object.prototype` with a `foo` property, then create a string and attempt to access the `foo` property as if it were a property of the string instance. Since the *myString* instance does not have a `foo` property, the prototype chain kicks in and the value is looked for at `String.prototype`. It is not there, so the next place to look is `Object.prototype`, which is the final location JavaScript will look for an object value. The `foo` value is found at `Object.prototype` because I added it, thus it returns the value of `foo`.

```
<!DOCTYPE html><html lang="en"><body><script>

Object.prototype.foo = 'foo';

var myString = 'bar';

// logs 'foo', being found at Object.prototype.foo via prototype chain
console.log(myString.foo);

</script>
</body>
```

Note

Careful! Anything added to Object.prototype will show up in a for in loop and the prototype chain. Because of this, it's been said (*http://erik.eae.net/archives/2005/06/06/22.13.54/*) that changing Object.prototype is forbidden or verboten, as some might say.

CHAPTER 4

Function()

Conceptual Overview of Using Function() Objects

A function is a container of code statements that can be invoked using the parentheses
( ) operator. Parameters can be passed inside of the parentheses during invocation so
that the statements in the function can access certain values when the function is
invoked.

Below, we create two versions of an addNumbers function object—one using the new
operator and another using the more common, literal pattern. Both are expecting two
parameters. In each case, we invoke the function, passing parameters in the parentheses
( ) operator.

Live Code (*http://jsfiddle.net/javascriptenlightenment/dMrDk/*)

```
<!DOCTYPE html><html lang="en"><body><script>

var addNumbersA = new Function('num1', 'num2', 'return num1 + num2');

console.log(addNumbersA(2, 2)); // logs 4

// could also be written the literal way, which is much more common
var addNumbersB = function(num1, num2) {return num1 + num2;};

console.log(addNumbersB(2, 2)); // logs 4

</script></body></html>
```

A function can be used to return a value, construct an object, or as a mechanism to
simply run code. JavaScript has several uses for functions, but in its most basic form, a
function is simply a unique scope of executable statements.

Function() Parameters

The `Function()` constructor takes an indefinite number of parameters, but the last parameter expected by the `Function()` constructor is a string containing statements that comprise the body of the function. Any parameters passed to the constructor before the last will be available to the function being created. It's also possible to send multiple parameters as a comma-separated string.

Below, I contrast the usage of the `Function()` constructor with the more common patterns of instantiating a function object.

Live Code (*http://jsfiddle.net/javascriptenlightenment/RT8QD/*)

```
<!DOCTYPE html><html lang="en"><body><script>


var addFunction = new Function('num1', 'num2', 'return num1 + num2');

/* Alternately, a single comma-separated string with arguments can be
   the first parameter of the constructor, with the function body following. */
var timesFunction = new Function('num1,num2', 'return num1 * num2');

console.log(addFunction(2,2),timesFunction(2,2)); // logs '4 4'

// versus the more common patterns for instantiating a function
var addFunction = function(num1, num2) {return num1 + num2;}; // expression form
function addFunction(num1, num2) {return num1 + num2;} // statement form


</script></body></html>
```

Notes

- Directly leveraging the `Function()` constructor is not recommended or typically ever done because JavaScript will use `eval()` to parse the string containing the function's logic. Many consider `eval()` to be unnecessary overhead. If it's in use, a flaw in the design of the code is highly possible.

- Using the `Function()` constructor without the `new` keyword has the same effect as using only the constructor to create function objects [e.g., `new Function('x','return x')` versus `function(('x','return x'))`].

- No closure is created (see Chapter 7) when invoking the `Function()` constructor directly.

Function() Properties and Methods

The function object has the following properties (not including inherited properties and methods):

Properties (e.g., `Function.prototype;`):

- `prototype`

Function Object Instance Properties and Methods

Function object instances have the following properties and methods:

Instance Properties (e.g., `var myFunction = function(x, y, z) {}; myFunc tion.length;`):

- `arguments`
- `constructor`
- `length`

Instance Methods (e.g., `var myFunction = function(x, y, z) {}; myFunction.to String();`):

- `apply()`
- `call()`
- `toString()`

Functions Always Return a Value

While it's possible to create a function simply to execute code statements, it's also very common for a function to return a value. Below, we are returning a string from the `sayHi` function.

Live Code (*http://jsfiddle.net/javascriptenlightenment/G6YrQ/*)

```
<!DOCTYPE html><html lang="en"><body><script>

var sayHi = function() {
    return 'Hi';
};

console.log(sayHi()); // logs "Hi"

</script></body></html>
```

If a function does not specify a return value, then undefined is returned. Below, we call the yelp function, which logs the string 'yelp' to the console without explicitly returning a value.

Live Code (*http://jsfiddle.net/javascriptenlightenment/LbenJ/*)

```
<!DOCTYPE html><html lang="en"><body><script>

var yelp = function() {
   console.log('I am yelping!');
   // functions return undefined even if we don't
}

/* logs true because a value is always returned,
even if we don't specifically return one */
console.log(yelp() === undefined);

</script></body></html>
```

The takeaway here is that all functions return a value, even if you do not explicitly provide a value to return. If you do not specify a value to return, the value returned is undefined.

Functions Are First-Class Citizens (Not Just Syntax but Values)

In JavaScript, functions are objects. This means that a function can be stored in a variable, array, or object. Also, a function can be passed to, and returned from, a function. A function has properties because it is an object. All of these factors make functions first-class citizens in JavaScript.

Live Code (*http://jsfiddle.net/javascriptenlightenment/2BTjU/*)

```
<!DOCTYPE html><html lang="en"><body><script>

/* functions can be stored in variables (funcA), arrays (funcB),
and objects (funcC) */
var funcA = function(){}; // called like so: funcA()
var funcB = [function(){}]; // called like so: funcB[0]()
var funcC = {method: function(){}}; // too.method() or funcC['method']()

// functions can be sent to, and sent back from, functions
var funcD = function(func){
   return func
};

var runFuncPassedToFuncD = funcD(function(){console.log('Hi');});

runFuncPassedToFuncD();
```

```
// functions are objects, which means they can have properties
var funcE = function(){};
funcE.answer = 'yup'; // instance property
console.log(funcE.answer); // logs 'yup'

</script></body></html>
```

It is crucial that you realize a function is an object, and thus a value. It can be passed around or augmented like any other expression in JavaScript.

Passing Parameters to a Function

Parameters are vehicles for passing values into the scope of a function when it is invoked. Below, as we invoke addFunction( ), since we have predefined it to take two parameters, two added values become available within its scope.

Live Code (*http://jsfiddle.net/javascriptenlightenment/MBhkj/*)

```
<!DOCTYPE html><html lang="en"><body><script>

var addFunction = function(number1, number2) {
    var sum = number1 + number2;
    return sum;
}

console.log(addFunction(3, 3)); // logs 6

</script></body></html>
```

Notes

- In contrast to some other programming languages, it is perfectly legal in JavaScript to omit parameters even if the function has been defined to accept these arguments. The missing parameters are simply given the value of undefined. Of course, by leaving out values for the parameters, the function might not work properly.

- If you pass unexpected parameters to a function (those not defined when the function was created), no error will occur. And it's possible to access these parameters from the arguments object, which is available to all functions.

this and arguments Values Available To All Functions

Inside the scope/body of all functions, the this and arguments values are available.

The `arguments` object is an array-like object containing all of the parameters being passed to the function. In the code below, even though we forgo specifying parameters when defining the function, we can rely on the `arguments` array passed to the function to access parameters if they are sent upon invocation.

Live Code (*http://jsfiddle.net/javascriptenlightenment/2R2Vz/*)

```
<!DOCTYPE html><html lang="en"><body><script>

var add = function() {
    return arguments[0] + arguments[1];
};

console.log(add(4, 4)); // returns 8

</script></body></html>
```

The `this` keyword, passed to all functions, is a reference to the object that contains the function. As you might expect, functions contained within objects as properties (i.e., methods) can use `this` to gain a reference to the "parent" object. When a function is defined in the global scope, the value of `this` is the global object. Review the code below and make sure you understand what `this` is returning.

Live Code (*http://jsfiddle.net/javascriptenlightenment/WFzW3/*)

```
<!DOCTYPE html><html lang="en"><body><script>

var myObject1 = {
    name: 'myObject1',
    myMethod: function(){console.log(this);}
};

myObject1.myMethod(); // logs 'myObject1'

var myObject2 = function(){console.log(this);};

myObject2(); // logs window

</script></body></html>
```

The arguments.callee Property

The `arguments` object has a property called `callee`, which is a reference to the function currently executing. This property can be used to reference the function from within the scope of the function (e.g., `arguments.callee`)—a self-reference. In the code below, we use this property to gain a reference to the calling function.

Live Code (*http://jsfiddle.net/javascriptenlightenment/TdZVg/*)

```
<!DOCTYPE html><html lang="en"><body><script>

var foo = function foo() {
   console.log(arguments.callee); // logs foo()
   /* callee could be used to invoke recursively the foo function
   (e.g., arguments.callee()) */
}();

</script></body></html>
```

This can be useful when a function needs to be called recursively.

The Function Instance length Property and arguments.length

The `arguments` object has a unique `length` property. While you might think this length property will give you the number of defined arguments, it actually gives the number of parameters sent to the function during invocation.

Live Code (*http://jsfiddle.net/javascriptenlightenment/CbgrD/*)

```
<!DOCTYPE html><html lang="en"><body><script>

var myFunction = function(z, s, d) {
   return arguments.length;
};

console.log(myFunction()); /* logs 0 because no parameters were passed
                              to the function */

</script></body></html>
```

Using the `length` property of all `Function()` instances, we can actually grab the total number of parameters the function is expecting.

Live Code (*http://jsfiddle.net/javascriptenlightenment/Uhjbb/*)

```
<!DOCTYPE html><html lang="en"><body><script>

var myFunction = function(z, s, d, e, r, m, q) {
   return myFunction.length;
};

console.log(myFunction()); // logs 7

</script></body></html>
```

Note

The `arguments.length` property beginning with JavaScript 1.4 is deprecated, and the number of arguments sent to a function can be accessed from the `length` property of the function object. So, moving forward, you can get the length value by leveraging the `callee` property to first gain reference to the function being invoked (i.e., `arguments.call ee.length`).

Redefining Function Parameters

A function's parameters can be redefined inside the function either directly, or by using the `arguments` array. Take a look at the code below.

Live Code (*http://jsfiddle.net/javascriptenlightenment/bE7cn/*)

```
<!DOCTYPE html><html lang="en"><body><script>

var foo = false;
var bar = false;

var myFunction = function(foo, bar) {
    arguments[0] = true;
    bar = true;
    console.log(arguments[0], bar); // logs true true
}

myFunction();

</script></body></html>
```

Notice that I can redefine the value of the *bar* parameter using the `arguments` index or by directly reassigning a new value to the parameter.

Return a Function Before It Is Done (Cancel Function Execution)

Functions can be cancelled at any time during invocation by using the `return` keyword with or without a value. Below, we are canceling the `add` function if the parameters are undefined or not a number.

Live Code (*http://jsfiddle.net/javascriptenlightenment/FQUje/*)

```
<!DOCTYPE html><html lang="en"><body><script>

var add = function(x, y) {
    // If the parameters are not numbers, return error.
    if (typeof x !== 'number' || typeof y !== 'number') {return 'pass in numbers';}
```

```
    return x + y;
}
console.log(add(3,3)); // logs 6
console.log(add('2','2')); // logs 'pass in numbers'

</script></body></html>
```

The takeaway here is that you can cancel a function's execution by using the `return` keyword at any point in the execution of the function.

Defining a Function (Statement, Expression, or Constructor)

A function can be defined in three different ways: a function constructor, a function statement, or a function expression. Below, I demonstrate each variation.

Live Code (*http://jsfiddle.net/javascriptenlightenment/DLrAk/*)

```
<!DOCTYPE html><html lang="en"><body><script>

/* function constructor: the last parameter is the function logic,
   everything before it is a parameter */
var addConstructor = new Function('x', 'y', 'return x + y');

// function statement
function addStatement(x, y) {
    return x + y;
}

// function expression
var addExpression = function(x, y) {
    return x + y;
};

console.log(addConstructor(2,2), addStatement (2,2), addExpression (2,2));
  // logs '4 4 4'

</script></body></html>
```

Note
Some have said that there is a fourth type of definition for functions, called the "named function expression." A named function expression is simply a function expression that also contains a name (e.g., `var add = function **add**(x, y) {return x+y})`.

Invoking a Function [Function, Method, Constructor, or call() and apply()]

Functions are invoked using four different scenarios or patterns:

- As a function
- As a method
- As a constructor
- Using apply() or call()

In the code below, we examine each of these invocation patterns.

Live Code (*http://jsfiddle.net/javascriptenlightenment/aqbQ9/*)

```
<!DOCTYPE html><html lang="en"><body><script>

// function pattern
var myFunction = function(){return 'foo'};
console.log(myFunction()); // log 'foo'

// method pattern
var myObject = {myFunction: function(){return 'bar';}}
console.log(myObject.myFunction()); // log 'bar'

// constructor pattern
var Cody = function(){
    this.living = true;
    this.age = 33;
    this.gender = 'male';
    this.getGender = function() {return this.gender;};
}
var cody = new Cody(); // invoke via Cody constructor
console.log(cody); // logs cody object and properties

// apply() and call() pattern
var greet = {
    runGreet: function(){
        console.log(this.name,arguments[0],arguments[1]);
    }
}

var cody = {name:'cody'};
var lisa = {name:'lisa'};

// invoke the runGreet function as if it were inside of the cody object
greet.runGreet.call(cody,'foo','bar'); // logs 'cody foo bar'

// invoke the runGreet function as if it were inside of the lisa object
greet.runGreet.apply(lisa, ['foo','bar']); // logs 'lisa foo bar'
```

```
/* Notice the difference between call() and apply() in how parameters are sent
to the function being invoked */
```

```
</script></body></html>
```

Make sure you are aware of all four of the invocation patterns, as code you will encounter may contain any of them.

Anonymous Functions

An anonymous function is a function that is not given an identifier. Anonymous functions are mostly used for passing functions as a parameter to another function.

Live Code (*http://jsfiddle.net/javascriptenlightenment/4nAX5/*)

```
<!DOCTYPE html><html lang="en"><body><script>

// function(){console.log('hi');}; // anonymous function, but no way to invoke it

// create a function that can invoke our anonymous function
var sayHi = function(f){
    f(); // invoke anonymous function
}

// pass an anonymous function as parameter
sayHi(function(){console.log('hi');}); // log 'hi'

</script></body></html>
```

Self-Invoking Function Expression

A function expression (really any function except one created from the `Function()` constructor) can be immediately invoked after definition by using the parentheses operator. Below, we create a `sayWord()` function expression and then immediately invoke the function. This is considered to be a self-invoking function.

Live Code (*http://jsfiddle.net/javascriptenlightenment/w9jMG/*)

```
<!DOCTYPE html><html lang="en"><body><script>

var sayWord = function() {console.log('Word 2 yo mo!');}();
// logs 'Word 2 yo mo!'

</script></body></html>
```

Self-Invoking Anonymous Function Statements

It's possible to create an anonymous function statement that is self-invoked. This is called a self-invoking anonymous function. Below, we create several anonymous functions that are immediately invoked.

Live Code (*http://jsfiddle.net/javascriptenlightenment/yUwFG/*)

```
<!DOCTYPE html><html lang="en"><body><script>

// most commonly used/seen in the wild
(function(msg) {
   console.log(msg);
})('Hi');

// slightly different but achieving the same thing:
(function(msg) {
   console.log(msg)
}('Hi'));

// the shortest possible solution
!function sayHi(msg) {console.log(msg);}('Hi');

// FYI, this does NOT work!
// function sayHi() {console.log('hi');}();

</script></body></html>
```

Note

According to the ECMAScript standard, the parentheses around the function (or anything that transforms the function into an expression) are required if the function is to be invoked immediately.

Functions Can Be Nested

Functions can be nested inside of other functions indefinitely. Below, we encapsulate the goo function inside of the bar function, which is inside of the foo function.

Live Code (*http://jsfiddle.net/javascriptenlightenment/ZsHua/*)

```
<!DOCTYPE html><html lang="en"><body><script>

var foo = function() {
   var bar = function() {
       var goo = function() {
          console.log(this); // logs reference to head window object
       }();
```

```
    }();
}();
```

```
</script></body></html>
```

The simple takeaway here is that functions can be nested and that there is no limit to how deep the nesting can go.

Note

Remember, the value of this for nested functions will be the head object (e.g., window object in a web browser) in JavaScript 1.5, ECMAScript 3 Edition.

Passing Functions to Functions and Returning Functions from Functions

As previously mentioned, functions are first-class citizens in JavaScript. And since a function is a value, and a function can be passed any sort of value, a function can be passed to a function. Functions that take and/or return other functions are sometimes called "higher-order functions."

Below, we are passing an anonymous function to the foo function, which we then immediately return from the foo function. It is this anonymous function that the variable bar points to, since foo accepts and then returns the anonymous function.

Live Code (*http://jsfiddle.net/javascriptenlightenment/w2C75/*)

```
<!DOCTYPE html><html lang="en"><body><script>

// functions can be sent to, and sent back from, functions
var foo = function(f) {
    return f;
}

var bar = foo(function() {console.log('Hi');});

bar(); // logs 'Hi'

</script></body></html>
```

So when bar is invoked, it invokes the anonymous function that was passed to the foo() function, which is then passed back from the foo() function and referenced from the bar variable. All this is to showcase the fact that functions can be passed around just like any other value.

Invoking Function Statements Before They Are Defined (Function Hoisting)

A function statement can be invoked during execution before its actual definition. This is a bit odd, but you should be aware of it so you can leverage it, or at least know what's going on when you encounter it. Below, I invoke the sayYo() and sum() function statements before they are defined.

Live Code (*http://jsfiddle.net/javascriptenlightenment/7hvUw/*)

```
<!DOCTYPE html><html lang="en"><body><script>

// Example 1

var speak = function() {
    sayYo(); /* sayYo() has not been defined yet but it can still be invoked,
                logs 'yo' */
    function sayYo() {console.log('Yo');}
}(); // invoke

// Example 2

console.log(sum(2, 2)); /* invoke sum(), which is not defined yet,
                           but can still be invoked */
function sum(x, y) {return x + y;}

</script></body></html>
```

This happens because before the code runs, function statements are interpreted and added to the execution stack/context. Make sure you are aware of this as you use function statements.

Note

Functions, defined as "function expressions" are not hoisted—only "function statements" are hoisted.

A Function Can Call Itself (Recursion)

It's perfectly legitimate for a function to call itself. In fact, this is often used in well-known coding patterns. In the code below, we kick off the countDownFrom function, which then calls itself via the function name countDownFrom. Essentially, this creates a loop that counts down from 5 to 0.

```
<!DOCTYPE html><html lang="en"><body><script>

var countDownFrom = function countDownFrom(num) {
   console.log(num);
   num--; // change the parameter value
   if (num < 0){return false;} // if num < 0 return function with no recursion
   // could have also done arguments.callee(num) if it was an anonymous function
   countDownFrom(num);
};

countDownFrom(5); // kick off the function, which logs separately 5,4,3,2,1,0

</script></body></html>
```

You should be aware that it's not uncommon for a function to invoke itself (a.k.a. recursion) or to do so repetitively.

CHAPTER 5

The Head/Global Object

Conceptual Overview of the Head Object

JavaScript code, itself, must be contained within an object. As an example, when crafting JavaScript code for a web browser environment, JavaScript is contained and executed within the `window` object. This `window` object is considered to be the "head object," or sometimes confusingly referred to as "the global object." All implementations of JavaScript require the use of a single head object.

The head object is set up by JavaScript behind the scenes to encapsulate user-defined code and to house the native code with which JavaScript comes prepackaged. User-defined code is placed by JavaScript inside the head object for execution. Let's verify this as it pertains to a web browser.

Below, I am creating some JavaScript values and verifying the values are placed in the head `window` object.

Live Code (*http://jsbin.com/upotis/edit*)

```
<!DOCTYPE html><html lang="en"><body><script>

var myStringVar = 'myString';
var myFunctionVar = function() {};
myString = 'myString';
myFunction = function() {};

console.log('myStringVar' in window); // returns true
console.log('myFunctionVar' in window); // return true
console.log('myString' in window); // returns true
console.log('myFunction' in window); // return true

</script></body></html>
```

You should always be aware that when you write JavaScript, it will be written in the context of the head object. The remaining material in this chapter assumes you are aware that the term "head object" is synonymous with "global object."

Note
The head object is the highest scope/context available in a JavaScript environment.

Global Functions Contained Within the Head Object

JavaScript ships with some predefined functions. The following native functions are considered methods of the head object [e.g., in a web browser `window.parse Int('500')`]. You can think of these as ready-to-use functions/methods (of the head object) provided by JavaScript:

- `decodeURI()`
- `decodeURIComponent()`
- `encodeURI()`
- `encodeURIComponent()`
- `eval()`
- `isFinite()`
- `isNaN()`
- `parseFloat()`
- `parseInt()`

The Head Object versus Global Properties and Global Variables

Do not confuse the head object with global properties or global variables contained within the global scope. The head object is an object that contains all objects. The term "global properties" or "global variables" is used to refer to values directly contained inside the head object and are not specifically scoped to other objects. These values are considered global because no matter where code is currently executing, in terms of scope, all code has access (via the scope chain) to these global properties/variables.

Below, I place a `foo` property in the the global scope, then access this property from a different scope.

```
<!DOCTYPE html><html lang="en"><body><script>

var foo = 'bar'; /* foo is a global object and a property of the
                    head/window object */

var myApp = function() { // remember functions create scope
   var run = function() {
       // logs bar, foo's value is found via the scope chain in the head object
       console.log(foo);
   }();
}

myApp();

</script></body></html>
```

Had I placed the `foo` property outside of the global scope, the `console.log` function would return `undefined`. This is demonstrated in the next code example.

```
<!DOCTYPE html><html lang="en"><body><script>

var myFunction = function() {var foo = 'bar'}; /* foo is now in the scope of
                                                  myFunction() */

var myApp = function() {
   var run = function() {
       console.log(foo); /* foo is undefined, no longer in the global scope,
                            error occurs */
   }();
}

myApp();

</script></body></html>
```

In the browser environment, this is why global property methods [e.g., `win dow.alert()`] can be invoked from any scope. What you need to take away from this is that anything in the global scope is available to any scope, and thus gets the title of "global variable" or "global property."

Note

There is a slight difference between using `var` and not using `var` in the global scope (global properties versus global variables). Have a look at this Stack Overflow exchange for the details (*http://stackoverflow.com/ questions/1470488/difference-between-using-var-and-not-using-var-in- javascript/1471738%231471738*).

Referring to the Head Object

There are typically two ways to reference the head object. The first way is to simply reference the name given to the head object (e.g., in a web browser this would be `win dow`). The second way is to use the `this` keyword in the global scope. Each of these are detailed in the code below.

Live Code (*http://jsbin.com/ubilim/edit*)

```
<!DOCTYPE html><html lang="en"><body><script>

var foo = 'bar';

windowRef1 = window;
windowRef2 = this;

console.log(windowRef1, windowRef2); // logs reference to window object

console.log(windowRef1.foo, windowRef2.foo); // logs 'bar', 'bar'

</script></body></html>
```

In the code above, we explicitly store a reference to the head object in two variables that are then used to gain access to the global `foo` variable.

The Head Object Is Implied and Typically Not Referenced Explicitly

Typically a reference to the head object is not used because it is implied. For example, in the browser environment, `window.alert` and `alert()` are essentially the same statement. JavaScript fills in the blanks here. Because the `window` object (i.e., the head object) is the last object checked in the scope chain for a value, the `window` object is essentially always implied. Below, we leverage the `alert()` function which is contained in the global scope.

Live Code (*http://jsbin.com/ikepup/edit*)

```
<!DOCTYPE html><html lang="en"><body><script>

var foo = { // window is implied here, window.foo
   fooMethod: function() {
       alert('foo' + 'bar'); // window is implied here, window.alert
       window.alert('foo' + 'bar'); /* window is explicitly used,
                                     with the same effect */
   }
}
```

```
foo.fooMethod(); // window is implied here, window.foo.fooMethod()

</script></body></html>
```

Make sure you understand that the head object is implied, even when you don't explicitly include it, because the head object is the last stop in the scope chain.

Note

Being explicit [e.g., window.alert() versus alert()] costs a little bit more with regards to performance (how fast the code runs). It's faster if you rely on the scope chain alone and avoid explicitly referencing the head object even if you know the property you want is contained in the global scope.

CHAPTER 6

The this Keyword

Conceptual Overview of this and How It Refers to Objects

When a function is created, a keyword called this is created (behind the scenes), which links to the object in which the function operates. Said another way, this is available to the scope of its function, yet is a reference to the object of which that function is a property/method.

Let's take a look at the cody object from Chapter 1 again:

Live Code (*http://jsfiddle.net/javascriptenlightenment/yMXec/*)

```
<!DOCTYPE html><html lang="en"><body><script>

var cody = {
    living : true,
    age : 23,
    gender : 'male',
    getGender : function() {return cody.gender;}
};

console.log(cody.getGender()); // logs 'male'

</script></body></html>
```

Notice how inside of the getGender function, we are accessing the gender property using dot notation (e.g., cody.gender) on the cody object itself. This can be rewritten using this to access the cody object because this points to the cody object.

Live Code (*http://jsfiddle.net/javascriptenlightenment/dDvPa/*)

```
<!DOCTYPE html><html lang="en"><body><script>

var cody = {
    living: true,
```

```
    age: 23,
    gender: 'male',
    getGender: function() {return this.gender;}
};

console.log(cody.getGender()); // logs 'male'

</script></body></html>
```

The this used in this.gender simply refers to the cody object on which the function is operating.

The topic of this can be confusing, but it does not have to be. Just remember that, in general, this is used inside of functions to refer to the object the function is contained within, as opposed to the function itself [exceptions include using the new keyword or call() and apply()].

Notes

- The keyword this looks and acts like any other variable, except you can't modify it.

- As opposed to arguments and any parameters sent to the function, this is a keyword (not a property) in the call/activation object.

How Is the Value of this Determined?

The value of this, passed to all functions, is based on the context in which the function is called at *runtime*. Pay attention here, because this is one of those quirks you just need to memorize.

The myObject object in the code below is given a property called sayFoo, which points to the sayFoo function. When the sayFoo function is called from the global scope, this refers to the window object. When it is called as a method of myObject, this refers to myObject.

Since myObject has a property named foo, that property is used.

Live Code (*http://jsbin.com/oxaliq/edit*)

```
<!DOCTYPE html><html lang="en"><body><script>

var foo = 'foo';
var myObject = {foo: 'I am myObject.foo'};

var sayFoo = function() {
    console.log(this['foo']);
};
```

```
// give myObject a sayFoo property and have it point to sayFoo function
myObject.sayFoo = sayFoo;

myObject.sayFoo(); // logs 'I am myObject.foo'
sayFoo(); // logs 'foo'

</script></body></html>
```

Clearly, the value of this is based on the *context* in which the function is being called. Consider that both myObject.sayFoo and sayFoo point to the same function. However, depending upon where (i.e., the context) sayFoo() is called from, the value of this is different.

If it helps, here is the same code with the head object (i.e., window) explicitly used.

Live Code (*http://jsfiddle.net/javascriptenlightenment/VeKWq/*)

```
<!DOCTYPE html><html lang="en"><body><script>

window.foo = 'foo';
window.myObject = {foo: 'I am myObject.foo'};

window.sayFoo = function() {
    console.log(this.foo);
};

window.myObject.sayFoo = window.sayFoo;

window.myObject.sayFoo();
window.sayFoo();

</script></body></html>
```

Make sure that as you pass around functions, or have multiple references to a function, you realize that the value of this will change depending upon the context in which you call the function.

Note

All variables except this and arguments follow lexical scope (*http://en.wikipedia.org/wiki/Lexical_scope%23Lexical_scoping*).

The this Keyword Refers to the Head Object in Nested Functions

You might be wondering what happens to this when it is used inside of a function that is contained inside of another function. The bad news is in ES3, this loses its way and refers to the head object (window object in browsers), instead of the object within which the function is defined.

In the code below, this inside of func2 and func3 loses its way and refers not to myObject but instead to the head object.

Live Code (http://jsfiddle.net/javascriptenlightenment/9GJhu/)

```
<!DOCTYPE html><html lang="en"><body><script>

var myObject = {
    func1: function() {
        console.log(this); // logs myObject
        var func2 = function() {
            console.log(this) // logs window, and will do so from this point on
            var func3 = function() {
                console.log(this); // logs window, as it's the head object
            }();
        }();
    }
}

myObject.func1();

</script></body></html>
```

The good news is that this will be fixed in ES5. For now, you should be aware of this predicament, especially when you start passing functions around as values to other functions.

Consider the code below and what happens when passing an anonymous function to foo.func1. When the anonymous function is called inside of foo.func1 (a function inside of a function) the this value inside of the anonymous function will be a reference to the head object.

Live Code (http://jsfiddle.net/javascriptenlightenment/DudU3/)

```
<!DOCTYPE html><html lang="en"><body><script>

var foo = {
    func1:function(bar) {
        bar(); // logs window, not foo
        console.log(this); /* the this keyword here will be a reference to
                            foo object */
    }
```

```
        }

        foo.func1(function(){console.log(this)});

</script></body></html>
```

Now you will never forget: the this value will always be a reference to the head object when its host function is encapsulated inside of another function or invoked within the context of another function (again, this is fixed in ES5).

Working Around the Nested Function Issue by Leveraging the Scope Chain

So that the this value does not get lost, you can simply use the scope chain to keep a reference to this in the parent function. The code below demonstrates how, using a variable called that, and leveraging its scope, we can keep better track of function context.

Live Code (*http://jsfiddle.net/javascriptenlightenment/k8uCu/*)

```
<!DOCTYPE html><html lang="en"><body><script>

var myObject = {
    myProperty: 'I can see the light',
    myMethod : function(){
        var that = this; /* store a reference to this (i.e., myObject)
                            in myMethod scope */
        var helperFunction function() { // child function
            // logs 'I can see the light' via scope chain because that = this
            console.log(that.myProperty); // logs 'I can see the light'
            console.log(this); // logs window object, if we don't use "that"
        }();
    }
}

myObject.myMethod(); // invoke myMethod

</script></body></html>
```

Controlling the Value of this Using call() or apply()

The value of this is normally determined from the context in which a function is called (except when the new keyword is used—more about that in a minute), but you can overwrite/control the value of this using apply() or call()to define what object this points to when invoking a function. Using these methods is like saying: "Hey, call X function but tell the function to use Z object as the value for this." By doing so, the default way in which JavaScript determines the value of this is overridden.

Below, we create an object and a function. We then invoke the function via `call()` so that the value of `this` inside the function uses `myObject` as its context. The statements inside the `myFunction` function will then populate `myObject` with properties instead of populating the head object. We have altered the object to which `this` (inside of `myFunction`) refers.

Live Code (*http://jsfiddle.net/javascriptenlightenment/7t6xD/*)

```html
<!DOCTYPE html><html lang="en"><body><script>

var myObject = {};

var myFunction = function(param1, param2) {
    // set via call() 'this' points to myObject when function is invoked
    this.foo = param1;
    this.bar = param2;
    console.log(this) // logs Object {foo = 'foo', bar = 'bar'}
};

myFunction.call(myObject, 'foo', 'bar'); /* invoke function, set this value to
                                            myObject */

console.log(myObject) // logs Object {foo = 'foo', bar = 'bar'}

</script></body></html>
```

In the example above, we are using `call()`, but `apply()` could be used as well. The difference between the two is how the parameters for the function are passed. Using `call()`, the parameters are just comma-separated values. Using `apply()`, the parameter values are passed inside of an array. Below, is the same idea, but using `apply()`.

Live Code (*http://jsfiddle.net/javascriptenlightenment/X9vDB/*)

```html
<!DOCTYPE html><html lang="en"><body><script>

var myObject = {};

var myFunction = function(param1, param2) {
    // set via apply(), this points to myObject when function is invoked
    this.foo = param1;
    this.bar = param2;
    console.log(this) // logs Object {foo = 'foo', bar = 'bar'}
};

myFunction.apply(myObject, ['foo', 'bar']); // invoke function, set this value

console.log(myObject) // logs Object {foo = 'foo', bar = 'bar'}

</script></body></html>
```

What you need to take away here is that you can override the default way in which JavaScript determines the value of `this` in a function's scope.

Using the this Keyword Inside a User-Defined Constructor Function

When a function is invoked with the `new` keyword, the value of `this`—as it's stated in the constructor—refers to the instance itself. Said another way: in the constructor function, we can leverage the object via `this` *before the object is actually created*. In this case, the default value of `this` changes in a way not unlike using `call()` or `apply()`.

Below, we set up a *Person* constructor function that uses `this` to reference an object being created. When an instance of *Person* is created, *this.name* will reference the newly created object and place a property called *name* in the new object with a value from the parameter (*name*) passed to the constructor function.

Live Code (*http://jsfiddle.net/javascriptenlightenment/TWecy/*)

```
<!DOCTYPE html><html lang="en"><body><script>

var Person = function(name) {
    this.name = name || 'john doe'; // this will refer to the instance created
}

var cody = new Person('Cody Lindley'); /* create an instance,
                                           based on Person constructor */

console.log(cody.name); // logs 'Cody Lindley'

</script></body></html>
```

Again, `this` refers to the "object that is to be" when the constructor function is invoked using the `new` keyword. Had we not used the `new` keyword, the value of `this` would be the context in which Person is invoked—in this case the head object. Let's examine this scenario.

Live Code (*http://jsfiddle.net/javascriptenlightenment/HHJ7y/*)

```
<!DOCTYPE html><html lang="en"><body><script>

var Person = function(name) {
    this.name = name || 'john doe';
}

var cody = Person('Cody Lindley'); // notice we did not use 'new'

console.log(cody.name); // undefined, the value is actually set at window.name
```

```
console.log(window.name); // logs 'Cody Lindley'

</script></body></html>
```

The this Keyword Inside a Prototype Method Refers to a Constructor Instance

When used in functions added to a constructor's `prototype` property, `this` refers to the instance on which the method is invoked. Say we have a custom `Person()` constructor function. As a parameter, it requires the person's full name. In case we need to access the full name of the person, we add a `whatIsMyFullName` method to the `Person.proto type`, so that all Person instances inherit the method. When using `this`, the method can refer to the instance invoking it (and thus its properties).

Here I demonstrate the creation of two Person objects (`cody` and `lisa`) and the inherited `whatIsMyFullName` method that contains the `this` keyword to access the instance.

Live Code (*http://jsfiddle.net/javascriptenlightenment/uV3sP/*)

```
<!DOCTYPE html><html lang="en"><body><script>

var Person = function(x){
    if(x){this.fullName = x};
};

Person.prototype.whatIsMyFullName = function(){
    return this.fullName; // 'this' refers to the instance created from Person()
}

var cody = new Person('cody lindley');
var lisa = new Person('lisa lindley');

/* call the inherited whatIsMyFullName method, which uses this to refer to
the instance */
console.log(cody.whatIsMyFullName(),lisa.whatIsMyFullName());

/* The prototype chain is still in effect, so if the instance does not have a
fullName property, it will look for it in the prototype chain. Below, we add
a fullName property to both the Person prototype and the Object prototype.
See notes. */

Object.prototype.fullName = 'John Doe';
var john = new Person(); // no argument is passed,
                         // so fullName is not added to instance
console.log(john.whatIsMyFullName()); // logs 'John Doe'

</script></body></html>
```

The takeaway here is that the keyword this is used to refer to instances when used inside of a method contained in the prototype object. If the instance does not contain the property, the prototype lookup begins.

Note

If the instance or the object pointed to by this does not contain the property being referenced, the same rules that apply to any property lookup get applied and the property will be "looked up" on the prototype chain. So in our example, if the fullName property was not contained within our instance, then fullName would be looked for at Person.prototype.fullName, and then Object.prototype.fullName.

CHAPTER 7

Scope and Closures

Conceptual Overview of JavaScript Scope

In JavaScript, scope is the context in which code is executed, and there are three types of scope: global scope, local scope (sometimes referred to as "function scope"), and eval scope.

Code defined using `var` inside of a function is locally scoped, and is only "visible" to other expressions in that function, which includes code inside any nested/child functions. Variables defined in the global scope can be accessed from anywhere because it is the highest level/last stop in the scope chain.

Examine the code below and make sure you understand that each declaration of `foo` is unique because of scope.

Live Code (*http://jsfiddle.net/javascriptenlightenment/RNLm3/*)

```
<!DOCTYPE html><html lang="en"><body><script>

var foo = 0; // global scope
console.log(foo); // logs 0

var myFunction = function() {

    var foo = 1; // local scope

    console.log(foo); // logs 1

    var myNestedFunction = function() {

        var foo = 2; // local scope

        console.log(foo); // logs 2
    }();
```

```
}();

eval('var foo = 3; console.log(foo);'); // eval() scope

</script></body></html>
```

Please notice that each foo variable contains a different value because each one is defined in a specifically delineated scope.

Notes

- An unlimited number of function and eval scopes can be created, while only one global scope is used by a JavaScript environment.
- The global scope is the last stop in the scope chain.
- Functions that contain functions create stacked execution scopes. These stacks which are chained together are often referred to as the scope chain.

JavaScript Does Not Have Block Scope

Since logic statements (e.g., if(){}) and looping statements (e.g., for) do not create a scope, variables can overwrite each other. Examine the code below and make sure you understand that the value of foo is being redefined as the program executes the code.

Live Code (*http://jsfiddle.net/javascriptenlightenment/Wn9p6/*)

```
<!DOCTYPE html><html lang="en"><body><script>

var foo = 1; // foo = 1

if (true) {
    foo = 2; // foo = 2
    for(var i = 3; i <= 5; i++) {
        foo = i; // foo = 3,4, then 5
        console.log(foo); // logs 3,4,5
    }
}

</script></body></html>
```

So foo is changing as the code executes because JavaScript has no block scope—only function, global, or eval scope.

Use var Inside Functions to Declare Variables and Avoid Scope Gotchas

JavaScript will declare any variables lacking a var declaration (even those contained in a function or encapsulated functions) to be in the global scope instead of the intended local scope. Have a look at the code below and notice that without the use of var to declare bar, the variable is actually defined in the global scope and not the local scope, where it should be.

Live Code (http://jsfiddle.net/javascriptenlightenment/WysKZ/)

```
<!DOCTYPE html><html lang="en"><body><script>

var foo = function() {
    var boo = function() {
        bar = 2; /* no var used, so bar is placed in the global scope
                    at window.bar */
    }();
}();

console.log(bar); // logs 2, because bar is in the global scope

// As opposed to...

var foo = function() {
    var boo = function() {
        var doo = 2;
    }();
}();

console.log(doo); /* logs undefined, doo is in the boo function scope,
                    error occurs */

</script></body></html>
```

The takeaway here is that you should always use var when defining variables inside of a function. This will prevent you from dealing with potentially confusing scope problems. The exception to this convention, of course, is when you want to create or change properties in the global scope from within a function.

The Scope Chain (Lexical Scoping)

There is a lookup chain that is followed when JavaScript looks for the value associated with a variable. This chain is based on the hierarchy of scope. In the code below, I am logging the value of sayHiText from the func2 function scope.

Live Code (*http://jsfiddle.net/javascriptenlightenment/2CNwT/*)

```
<!DOCTYPE html><html lang="en"><body><script>

var sayHiText = 'howdy';

var func1 = function() {
   var func2 = function() {
       console.log(sayHiText); /* func2 scope, but it finds sayHiText in
                                  global scope */
   }();
}();

</script></body></html>
```

How is the value of sayHiText found when it is not contained inside of the scope of the func2 function? JavaScript first looks in the func2 function for a variable named say HiText. Not finding func2 there, it looks up to func2's parent function, func1. The *sayHiText* variable is not found in the func1 scope, either, so JavaScript then continues up to the global scope where sayHiText is found, at which point the value of sayHi Text is delivered. If sayHiText had not been defined in the global scope, undefined would have been returned by JavaScript.

This is such an important concept to grok. Let's examine another code example. Below, we grab three values from three different scopes.

Live Code (*http://jsfiddle.net/javascriptenlightenment/Uv66Q/*)

```
<!DOCTYPE html><html lang="en"><body><script>

var x = 10;
var foo = function() {
   var y = 20;
   var bar = function() {
       var z = 30;
       console.log(z + y + x); // z is local, y and z are found in the scope chain
   }();
}()

foo(); // logs 60

</script></body></html>
```

The value for z is local to the bar function and the context in which the console.log is invoked, the value for y is in the foo function, which is the parent of bar(), and the value for x is in the global scope. All of these are accessible to the bar function via the scope chain. Make sure you understand that referencing variables in the bar function will check all the way up the scope chain for the variables referenced.

Note
The scope chain, if you think about it, is not that different from the prototype chain. Both are simply a way for a value to be looked up by checking a systematic and hierarchical set of locations.

The Scope Chain Lookup Returns the First Found Value

In the code below, a variable called x exists in the same scope in which it is examined with console.log. This "local" value of x is used, and one might say that it shadows, or masks, the identically named x variables found further up in the scope chain.

Live Code (*http://jsfiddle.net/javascriptenlightenment/6BMPV/*)

```
<!DOCTYPE html><html lang="en"><body><script>

var x = false;
var foo = function() {
   var x = false;
   bar = function() {
       var x = true;
       console.log(x); // local x is first in the scope so it shadows the rest
   }();
}

foo(); // logs true

</script></body></html>
```

Remember that the scope lookup ends when the variable is found in the nearest available link of the chain, even if the same variable name is used further up the chain.

Scope Is Determined During Function Definition, not Invocation

Since functions determine scope and functions can be passed around just like any JavaScript value, one might think that deciphering the scope chain is complicated. It is actually very simple. The scope chain is decided based on the location of a function during *definition*, not during invocation. This is also called *lexical scoping*. Think long and hard about this, as most people stumble over it a lot in JavaScript code.

The scope chain is created before you invoke a function. Because of this, we can create closures. For example, we can have a function return a nested function to the global scope, yet our function can still access, via the scope chain, its parent function's scope.

Below, we define a `parentFunction` that returns an anonymous function, and we call the returned function from the global scope. Because our anonymous function was defined as being contained inside of `parentFunction`, it still has access to `parentFunc`tion's scope when it is invoked. This is called a closure.

Live Code (*http://jsfiddle.net/javascriptenlightenment/TCdbJ/*)

```
<!DOCTYPE html><html lang="en"><body><script>

var parentFunction = function() {
    var foo = 'foo';
    return function() { // anonymous function being returned
        console.log(foo); // logs 'foo'
    }
}

// nestedFunction refers to the nested function returned from parentFunction
var nestedFunction = parentFunction();

nestedFunction(); /* logs foo because the returned function accesses foo
                      via the scope chain */


</script></body></html>
```

What you should take away here is that the scope chain is determined during definition —literally in the way the code is written. Passing around functions inside of your code will not change the scope chain.

Closures Are Caused by the Scope Chain

Take what you have learned about the scope chain and scope lookup in this chapter, and a closure should not be overly complicated to understand. Below, we create a function called `countUpFromZero`. This function actually returns a reference to the child function contained within it. When this child function (nested function) is invoked, it still has access to the parent function's scope because of the scope chain.

Live Code (*http://jsfiddle.net/javascriptenlightenment/8u3Km/*)

```
<!DOCTYPE html><html lang="en"><body><script>

var countUpFromZero = function() {
    var count = 0;
    return function() { /* return nested child function when countUpFromZero is
                            invoked */
        return ++count; // count is defined up the scope chain, in parent function
    };
}(); // invoke immediately, return nested function
```

```
console.log(countUpFromZero()); // logs 1
console.log(countUpFromZero()); // logs 2
console.log(countUpFromZero()); // logs 3

</script></body></html>
```

Each time the countUpFromZero function is invoked, the anonymous function contained in (and returned from) the countUpFromZero function still has access to the parent function's scope. This technique, facilitated via the scope chain, is an example of a closure.

 Note

If you feel I have oversimplified closures, you are likely correct in this thought. But I did so on purpose, as I believe the important parts come from a solid understanding of functions and scope, not necessarily the complexities of execution context. If you are in need of an in-depth dive into closures, have a look at "JavaScript Closures" (*http://jibbering.com/faq/notes/closures/*).

CHAPTER 8

Function Prototype Property

Conceptual Overview of the Prototype Chain

The `prototype` property is an object created by JavaScript for every `Function()` instance. Specifically, it links object instances created with the `new` keyword back to the constructor function that created them. This is done so that instances can share, or inherit, common methods and properties. Importantly, the sharing occurs during property lookup. Remember from Chapter 1 that every time you look up or access a property on an object, the property will be searched for on the object as well as the prototype chain.

Note

A prototype object is created for every function, regardless of whether you intend to use that function as a constructor.

Below, I construct an array from the `Array()` constructor, and then I invoke the `join()` method.

Live Code (*http://jsfiddle.net/javascriptenlightenment/4L7ae/*)

```
<!DOCTYPE html><html lang="en"><body><script>

var myArray = new Array('foo', 'bar');

console.log(myArray.join()); // logs 'foo, bar'

</script></body></html>
```

The join() method is not defined as a property of the myArray object instance, but somehow we have access to join() as if it were. This method is defined somewhere, but where? Well, it is defined as a property of the Array() constructor's prototype property. Since join() is not found within the array object instance, JavaScript looks up the prototype chain for a method called join().

Okay, so why are things done this way? Really, it is about efficiency and reuse. Why should every array instance created from the array constructor function have a uniquely defined join() method when join() always functions the same way? It makes more sense for all arrays to leverage the same join() function without having to create a new instance of the function for each array instance.

This efficiency we speak of is all possible because of the prototype property, prototype linkage, and the prototype lookup chain. In this chapter, we break down these often confusing attributes of prototypal inheritance. But truth be told, you would be better off simply memorizing the mechanics of how the chain hierarchy actually works. Refer back to Chapter 1 if you need a refresher on how property values are resolved.

Why Care About the prototype Property?

You should care about the prototype property for four reasons.

1. The first reason is that the prototype property is used by the native constructor functions (e.g., Object(), Array(), Function(), etc.) to allow constructor instances to inherit properties and methods. It is the mechanism that JavaScript itself uses to allow object instances to inherit properties and methods from the constructor function's prototype property. If you want to understand JavaScript better, you need to understand how JavaScript itself leverages the prototype object.

2. When creating user-defined constructor functions, you can orchestrate inheritance the same way JavaScript native objects do. But first you have to grok how it works.

3. You might really dislike prototypal inheritance or prefer another pattern for object inheritance, but the reality is that someday you might have to edit or manage someone else's code who thought prototypal inheritance was the bee's knees. When this happens, you should be aware of how prototypal inheritance works, as well as how it can be replicated by developers who make use of custom constructor functions.

4. By using prototypal inheritance, you can create efficient object instances that all leverage the same methods. As already mentioned, not all array objects, which are instances of the Array() constructor, need their own join() methods. All instances can leverage the same join() method because the method is stored in the prototype chain.

Prototype Is Standard on All function() Instances

All functions are created from a Function() constructor, even if you do not directly invoke the Function() constructor (e.g., var add = new Function('x', 'y', 'return x + z');) and instead use the literal notation (e.g., var add = function(x,y) {return x + z};).

When a function instance is created, it is always given a prototype property, which is an empty object. Below, we define a function called myFunction, then we access the prototype property, which is simply an empty object.

Live Code (*http://jsfiddle.net/javascriptenlightenment/E5LKA/*)

```
<!DOCTYPE html><html lang="en"><body><script>

var myFunction = function() {};
console.log(myFunction.prototype); // logs object{}
console.log(typeof myFunction.prototype); // logs 'object'

</script></body></html>
```

Make sure you completely understand that the prototype property is coming from the Function() constructor. It is only once we intend to use our function as a user-defined constructor function that the prototype property is leveraged, but this does not change the fact that the Function() constructor gives each instance a prototype property.

The Default prototype Property Is an Object() Object

All this prototype talk can get a bit heavy. Truly, prototype is just an empty object property called "prototype" created behind the scenes by JavaScript and made available by invoking the Function() constructor. If you were to do it manually, it would look something like this:

Live Code (*http://jsfiddle.net/javascriptenlightenment/GxKLr/*)

```
<!DOCTYPE html><html lang="en"><body><script>

var myFunction = function() {};

myFunction.prototype = {}; /* add the prototype property and set it to an
                              empty object */

console.log(myFunction.prototype); // logs an empty object

</script></body></html>
```

In fact, the above code actually works just fine, essentially just duplicating what JavaScript already does.

Note
The value of a `prototype` property can be set to any of the complex values (i.e., objects) available in JavaScript. JavaScript will ignore any prototype property set to a primitive value.

Instances Created From a Constructor Function are Linked to the Constructor's prototype Property

While it's only an object, `prototype` is special because the prototype chain links every instance to its constructor function's `prototype` property. This means that any time an object is created from a constructor function using the `new` keyword (or when an object wrapper is created for a primitive value), it adds a hidden link between the object instance created and the `prototype` property of the constructor function used to create it. This link is known inside the instance as __proto__ (*http://mzl.la/QFxtgH*) [though it is only *exposed/supported* via code in Firefox 2+, Safari, Chrome, and Android]. JavaScript wires this together in the background when a constructor function is invoked and it's this link that allows the prototype chain to be, well, a chain. Below, we add a property to the native `Array()` constructor's `prototype`, which we can then access from an `Array()` instance using the __proto__ property set on that instance.

Live Code (*http://jsfiddle.net/javascriptenlightenment/kcz6q/*)

```
<!DOCTYPE html><html lang="en"><body><script>

// this code only works in browsers that supports __proto__ access

Array.prototype.foo = 'foo';
var myArray = new Array();
// Only works in Firefox 2+, Safari, Chrome, and Android

console.log(myArray.__proto__.foo); /* logs foo, because
                                    myArray.__proto__ = Array.prototype */

</script></body></html>
```

Since accessing __proto__ is not part of the official ECMA standard, there is a more universal way to trace the link from an object to the prototype object it inherits, and that is by using the `constructor` property. This is demonstrated below.

Live Code (*http://jsfiddle.net/javascriptenlightenment/2QLvv/*)

```
<!DOCTYPE html><html lang="en"><body><script>

Array.prototype.foo = 'foo'; /* all instances of Array() now inherit a
                              foo property */
var myArray = new Array();
```

```
// trace foo in a verbose way leveraging *.constructor.prototype
console.log(myArray.constructor.prototype.foo); // logs foo

// or, of course, leverage the chain
console.log(myArray.foo) // logs foo
// uses prototype chain to find property at Array.prototype.foo

</script></body></html>
```

In the code above, the foo property is found within the prototype object. You need to realize this is only possible because of the association/link between the instance of Array() and the Array() constructor prototype object (i.e., Array.prototype). Simply put, myArray.__proto__ (or myArray.constructor.prototype) references Array.prototype.

Last Stop in the prototype Chain is Object.prototype

Since the prototype property is an object, the last stop in the prototype chain or lookup is at Object.prototype. In the code below, I create myArray, which is an empty array. I then attempt to access a property of myArray which has not yet been defined, engaging the prototype lookup chain. The myArray object is examined for the foo property. Being absent, it then looks for the property at Array.prototype, but it is not there, either. So the final place it looks is Object.prototype. Because it is not defined in any of those three objects, the property is undefined.

Live Code (*http://jsfiddle.net/javascriptenlightenment/L6ZaS/*)

```
<!DOCTYPE html><html lang="en"><body><script>

var myArray = [];

console.log(myArray.foo) // logs undefined

/* foo was not found at myArray.foo or Array.prototype.foo or
Object.prototype.foo, so it is undefined. */

</script></body></html>
```

Take note that the chain stopped with Object.prototype. The last place we looked for foo was Object.prototype.

Note

Careful! Anything added to Object.prototype will show up in a for in loop.

The prototype Chain Returns the First Property Match It Finds in the Chain

Like the scope chain, the `prototype` chain will use the first value it finds during the chain lookup.

Modifying the last code example, if we added the same value to the `Object.proto type` and `Array.prototype` objects, and then attempted to access a value on an array instance, the value returned would be from the `Array.prototype` object.

Live Code (*http://jsfiddle.net/javascriptenlightenment/3cYUz/*)

```
<!DOCTYPE html><html lang="en"><body><script>

Object.prototype.foo = 'object-foo';
Array.prototype.foo = 'array-foo';
var myArray = [];

console.log(myArray.foo); // logs 'array-foo', was found at Array.prototype.foo

myArray.foo = 'bar';

console.log(myArray.foo) // logs 'bar', was found at Array.foo

</script></body></html>
```

In the code above, the foo value at `Array.prototype.foo` is shadowing, or masking, the foo value found at `Object.prototype.foo`. Just remember that the lookup ends when the property is found in the chain, even if the same property name is also used farther up the chain.

Replacing the prototype Property with a New Object Removes the Default Constructor Property

It's possible to replace the default value of a `prototype` property with a new value. Doing so, however, will eliminate the default *constructor* property found in the "pre-made" prototype object—unless you manually specify one.

In the code below, we create a `Foo` constructor function, replace the `prototype` property with a new empty object, and verify that the constructor property is broken (it now references the less useful `Object()` constructor).

Live Code (*http://jsfiddle.net/javascriptenlightenment/rWv8Z/*)

```
<!DOCTYPE html><html lang="en"><body><script>

var Foo = function Foo(){};
```

```
Foo.prototype = {}; // replace prototype property with an empty object

var FooInstance = new Foo();

console.log(FooInstance.constructor === Foo); /* logs false,
                                              we broke the reference */
console.log(FooInstance.constructor); // logs Object(), not Foo()

// compare to code where we do not replace the prototype value

var Bar = function Bar(){};

var BarInstance = new Bar();

console.log(BarInstance.constructor === Bar); // logs true
console.log(BarInstance.constructor); // logs Bar()

</script></body></html>
```

If you intend to replace the default `prototype` property (common with some JS OOP patterns) set up by JavaScript, you should wire back together a constructor property that references the constructor function. Below, we alter our previous code so that the `constructor` property will again provide a reference to the proper constructor function.

Live Code (*http://jsfiddle.net/javascriptenlightenment/uc389/*)

```
<!DOCTYPE html><html lang="en"><body><script>

var Foo = function Foo(){};

Foo.prototype = {constructor:Foo};

var FooInstance = new Foo();

console.log(FooInstance.constructor === Foo); // logs true
console.log(FooInstance.constructor); // logs Foo()

</script></body></html>
```

Instances That Inherit Properties from the Prototype Will Always Get the Latest Values

The `prototype` property is *dynamic* in the sense that instances will always get the latest value from the prototype, regardless of when it was instantiated, changed, or appended. In the code below, we create a Foo constructor, add the property x to the `prototype`, and then create an instance of Foo( ) named FooInstance. Next, we log the value of x. Then we update the prototype's value of x and log it again to find that our instance has access to the latest value found in the `prototype` object.

Live Code (*http://jsfiddle.net/javascriptenlightenment/mLyJQ/*)

```
<!DOCTYPE html><html lang="en"><body><script>

var Foo = function Foo(){};

Foo.prototype.x = 1;

var FooInstance = new Foo();

console.log(FooInstance.x); // logs 1

Foo.prototype.x = 2;

console.log(FooInstance.x); // logs 2, the FooInstance was updated

</script></body></html>
```

Given how the lookup chain works, this behavior should not be that surprising. If you are wondering, this works the same, regardless of whether you use the default proto type object or override it with your own. Here I replace the default prototype object to demonstrate this fact:

Live Code (*http://jsfiddle.net/javascriptenlightenment/xnyHk/*)

```
<!DOCTYPE html><html lang="en"><body><script>

var Foo = function Foo(){};

Foo.prototype = {x:1}; // the logs below still work the same

var FooInstance = new Foo();

console.log(FooInstance.x); // logs 1

Foo.prototype.x = 2;

console.log(FooInstance.x); // logs 2, the FooInstance was updated

</script></body></html>
```

Replacing the prototype Property with a New Object Does Not Update Former Instances

You might think that you can replace the prototype property entirely at any time and that all instances will be updated, but this is not correct. When you create an instance, that instance will be tied to the prototype that was "minted" at the time of instantiation. Providing a new object as the prototype property does not update the connection between instances already created and the new prototype.

But remember, as I stated above, you can *update* or *add to* the originally created proto type object and those values remain connected to the first instance(s).

Live Code (*http://jsfiddle.net/javascriptenlightenment/fQHJB/*)

```
<!DOCTYPE html><html lang="en"><body><script>

var Foo = function Foo(){};

Foo.prototype.x = 1;

var FooInstance = new Foo();

console.log(FooInstance.x); // logs 1, as you think it would

// now let's replace/override the prototype object with a new Object() object
Foo.prototype = {x:2};

console.log(FooInstance.x); /* logs 1, WHAT? Shouldn't it log 2, we just
                               updated prototype */
/* FooInstance still references the same state of the prototype object that
was there when it was instantiated. */

// create a new instance of Foo()
var NewFooInstance = new Foo();

// the new instance is now tied to the new prototype object value (i.e., {x:2};)
console.log(NewFooInstance.x); // logs 2

</script></body></html>
```

The key takeaway here is that an object's prototype should not be replaced with a new object once you start creating instances. Doing so will result in instances that have a link to different prototypes.

User-Defined Constructors Can Leverage the Same Prototype Inheritance as Native Constructors

Hopefully at this point in the chapter it is sinking in how JavaScript itself leverages the prototype property for inheritance (e.g., Array.prototype). This same pattern can be leveraged when creating non-native, user-defined constructor functions. Below, we take the classic Person object and mimic the pattern that JavaScript uses for inheritance.

Live Code (*http://jsfiddle.net/javascriptenlightenment/7SBmx/*)

```
<!DOCTYPE html><html lang="en"><body><script>

var Person = function() {};
```

```
// all Person instances inherit a legs, arms, and countLimbs properties
Person.prototype.legs = 2;
Person.prototype.arms = 2;
Person.prototype.countLimbs = function() {return this.legs + this.arms;};

var chuck = new Person();

console.log(chuck.countLimbs()); // logs 4

</script></body></html>
```

In the code above, a `Person()` constructor function is created. We then add properties to the `prototype` property of `Person()`, which can be inherited by all instances. So clearly, in your code you can leverage the prototype chain the same way that JavaScript leverages it for native object inheritance.

As a good example of how you might leverage this, you can create a constructor function whose instances inherit *legs* and *arms* properties if they are not provided as parameters. Below, if the `Person()` constructor is sent parameters, they are used as instance properties, but if one or more parameters is not provided, there is a fallback. These instance properties then shadow or mask the inherited properties. So you have the best of both worlds.

Live Code (*http://jsfiddle.net/javascriptenlightenment/BmeEA/*)

```
<!DOCTYPE html><html lang="en"><body><script>

var Person = function(legs, arms) {

    // shadow prototype value
    if (legs !== undefined) {this.legs = legs;}
    if (arms !== undefined) {this.arms = arms;}
};

Person.prototype.legs = 2;
Person.prototype.arms = 2;
Person.prototype.countLimbs = function() {return this.legs + this.arms;};

var chuck = new Person(0, 0);

console.log(chuck.countLimbs()); // logs 0

</script></body></html>
```

Creating Inheritance Chains (the Original Intention)

Prototypal inheritance was conceived to allow inheritance chains that mimic the inheritance patterns found in traditional *object-oriented programming* languages. Inheritance is simply one object being given access to another object's properties. This is done by instantiating an instance of the object you want to inherit from as the value for the `prototype` property of the function that creates the object that is doing the inheriting. When this is done, there is a link (a.k.a. __proto__) between the objects that extends the available properties to an object upon property lookup.

In the code below, Chef objects (i.e., `cody`) inherit from `Person()`. This means that if a property is not found in a Chef object, it will next be looked for on the prototype of the function that created `Person()` objects. To wire up the inheritance, all you have to do is instantiate an instance of `Person()` as the value for `Chef.prototype` (i.e., `Chef.prototype = new Person();`).

Live Code (*http://jsfiddle.net/javascriptenlightenment/rRbsL/*)

```
<!DOCTYPE html><html lang="en"><body><script>

var Person = function(){this.bar = 'bar'};
Person.prototype.foo = 'foo';

var Chef = function(){this.goo = 'goo'};
Chef.prototype = new Person();
var cody = new Chef();

console.log(cody.foo); // logs 'foo'
console.log(cody.goo); // logs 'goo'
console.log(cody.bar); // logs 'bar'

</script></body></html>
```

All we have done in the above code is to leverage a system that is already in place with the native objects. Consider that `Person()` is not unlike the default `Object()` value for `prototype` properties. In other words, this is exactly what happens when a `prototype` property, containing its default empty `Object()` value, looks to the prototype of the constructor function that created it (i.e., `Object.prototype`) for inherited properties.

CHAPTER 9

Array()

Conceptual Overview of Using Array() Objects

An array is an ordered list of values, typically created with the intention of looping through numerically indexed values, beginning with the index zero. What you need to know is that arrays are numerically ordered sets, versus objects, which have property names associated with values in non-numeric order. Essentially, arrays use numbers as a lookup key, while objects have user-defined property names. JavaScript does not have true associative arrays, but objects can be used to achieve the functionality of associate arrays.

Below, I store four strings in myArray that I can access using a numeric index. I compare and contrast it to an object-literal mimicking an associative array.

Live Code (*http://jsfiddle.net/javascriptenlightenment/TTL5E/*)

```
<!DOCTYPE html><html lang="en"><body><script>

var myArray = ['blue', 'green', 'orange', 'red'];

console.log(myArray[0]); // logs blue using 0 index to access string in myArray

// versus

var myObject = { // a.k.a. associative array/hash, known as an object in JavaScript
    'blue': 'blue',
    'green': 'green',
    'orange': 'orange',
    'red': 'red'
};

console.log(myObject['blue']); // logs blue

</script></body></html>
```

Notes

- Arrays can hold any type of values, and these values can be updated or deleted at any time.
- If you need a "hash" (a.k.a. associative array), an object is the closest solution.
- An `Array()` is just a special type of `Object()`. That is, `Array()` instances are basically `Object()` instances with a couple of extra functions (e.g., `.length` and a built-in numeric index).
- Values contained in an array are commonly referred to as elements.

Array() Parameters

You can pass the values of an array instance to the constructor as comma-separated parameters (e.g., `new Array('foo', 'bar');`). The `Array()` constructor can take up to 4,294,967,295 parameters.

However, if only one parameter is sent to the `Array()` constructor, and that value is an integer (e.g., 1, 123, or 1.0), then it will be used to set up the `length` of the array, and will not be used as a *value* contained within the array.

Live Code (*http://jsfiddle.net/javascriptenlightenment/TjABp/*)

```
<!DOCTYPE html><html lang="en"><body><script>

var foo = new Array(1, 2, 3);
var bar = new Array(100);

console.log(foo[0], foo[2]); // logs '1 3'
console.log(bar[0], bar.length); // logs 'undefined 100'

</script></body></html>
```

Array() Properties and Methods

The `Array()` object has the following properties (not including inherited properties and methods):

Properties (e.g., `Array.prototype`):

- `prototype`

Array Object Instance Properties and Methods

Array object instances have the following properties and methods:

Instance Properties (e.g., `var myArray = ['foo', 'bar']; myArray.length;`):

- constructor
- index
- input
- length

Instance Methods (e.g., `var myArray = ['foo']; myArray.pop();`):

- pop()
- push()
- reverse()
- shift()
- sort()
- splice()
- unshift()
- concat()
- join()
- slice()

Creating Arrays

Like most of the objects in JavaScript, an array object can be created using the new operator in conjunction with the `Array()` constructor, or by using the literal syntax.

Below, I create the `myArray1` array with predefined values using the `Array()` constructor, and then `myArray2` using literal notation.

Live Code (*http://jsfiddle.net/javascriptenlightenment/Gs8rR/*)

```
<!DOCTYPE html><html lang="en"><body><script>

// Array() constructor
var myArray1 = new Array('blue', 'green', 'orange', 'red');

console.log(myArray1); // logs ["blue", "green", "orange", "red"]
```

```
// array literal notation
var myArray2 = ['blue', 'green', 'orange', 'red'];

console.log(myArray2); // logs ["blue", "green", "orange", "red"]

</script></body></html>
```

It is more common to see an array defined using the literal syntax, but one should be aware that this shortcut is merely concealing the use of the `Array()` constructor.

Notes

- In practice, the array literal is typically all you will ever need.
- Regardless of how an array is defined, if you do not provide any predefined values to the array, it will still be created but will simply contain no values.

Adding and Updating Values in Arrays

A value can be added to an array at any index, at any time. Below, we are adding a value to the numeric index 50 of an empty array. What about all the indexes before 50? Well, like I said, you can add a value to an array at any index, at any time. But, if you add a value to the numeric index 50 of an empty array, JavaScript will fill in all of the necessary indexes before it with `undefined` values.

Live Code (*http://jsfiddle.net/javascriptenlightenment/2VPSS/*)

```
<!DOCTYPE html><html lang="en"><body><script>

var myArray = [];
myArray[50] = 'blue';
console.log(myArray.length); /* logs 51 (0 is counted) because JS created
                               values 0 to 50 before "blue"*/

</script></body></html>
```

Additionally, considering the dynamic nature of JavaScript and the fact that JavaScript is not strongly typed, an array value can be updated at any time and the value contained in the index can be any legal JavaScript value. Below, I change the value at the numeric index 50 to an object.

Live Code (*http://jsfiddle.net/javascriptenlightenment/ZkqxK/*)

```
<!DOCTYPE html><html lang="en"><body><script>

var myArray = [];
myArray[50] = 'blue';
```

object type from string to
object */
{color="blue"}'

:he array, then the property blue
; 'blue'

blue'

eans that the first numeric slot to hold a
can be a bit confusing—if I create an array
0 while the length of the array is 1. Make
:ray represents the number of values con-
idex of the array starts at zero.

the myArray array at the numeric index 0,
but since the array contains one value, the length of the array is 1.

Live Code (*http://jsfiddle.net/javascriptenlightenment/8amEG/*)

```
<!DOCTYPE html><html lang="en"><body><script>

var myArray = ['blue'] // the index 0 contains the string value 'blue'
console.log(myArray[0]); // logs 'blue'
console.log(myArray.length); // logs 1

</script></body></html>
```

Defining Arrays with a Predefined Length

As I mentioned earlier, by passing a single integer parameter to the Array() constructor, it's possible to predefine the array's length, or the number of values it will contain. In this case, the constructor makes an exception and assumes you want to set the length of the array and not pre-populate the array with values.

Below, we set up the myArray array with a predefined length of 3. Again, we are configuring the *length* of the array, not passing it a value to be stored at the 0 index.

Live Code (*http://jsfiddle.net/javascriptenlightenment/SmgaZ/*)

```
<!DOCTYPE html><html lang="en"><body><script>

var myArray = new Array(3);
```

```
console.log(myArray.length); /* logs 3, because we are passing one
                                numeric parameter */
console.log(myArray[0]); // logs undefined

</script></body></html>
```

Notes

- Providing a predefined length will give each numeric index, up to the length specified, an associated value of undefined.
- You might be wondering if it is possible to create a predefined array containing only one numeric value. Yes, it is—by using the literal form var myArray = [4].

Setting Array Length can Add or Remove Values

The length property of an array object can be used to get or set the length of an array. As shown above, setting the length higher than the actual number of values contained in the array will add undefined values to the array. What you might not expect is that you can actually remove values from an array by setting the length value to a number less than the number of values contained in the array.

Live Code (*http://jsfiddle.net/javascriptenlightenment/ScQ5u/*)

```
<!DOCTYPE html><html lang="en"><body><script>

var myArray = ['blue', 'green', 'orange', 'red'];
console.log(myArray.length); // logs 4
myArray.length = 99;
console.log(myArray.length); /* logs 99, remember we set the length,
                                not an index */
myArray.length = 1; // removed all but one value, so index [1] is gone!
console.log(myArray[1]); // logs undefined

console.log(myArray); // logs '["blue"]'

</script></body></html>
```

Arrays Containing Other Arrays (Multidimensional Arrays)

Since an array can hold any valid JavaScript value, an array can contain other arrays. When this is done, the array containing encapsulated arrays is considered a *multidimensional* array. Accessing encapsulated arrays is done by *bracket chaining*. Below, we create an array literal that contains an array, inside of which we create another array literal, inside of which we create another array literal, containing a string value at the 0 index.

Live Code (*http://jsfiddle.net/javascriptenlightenment/eGPLR/*)

```
<!DOCTYPE html><html lang="en"><body><script>

var myArray = [[[['4th dimension']]]];
console.log(myArray[0][0][0][0]); // logs '4th dimension'

</script></body></html>
```

The code above is rather silly, but you can take away the fact that arrays can contain other arrays and you can access encapsulated arrays indefinitely.

Looping Over an Array, Backwards and Forwards

The simplest (and arguably the fastest) way to loop over an array is to use the `while` loop.

Below, we loop from the beginning of the index to the end.

Live Code (*http://jsfiddle.net/javascriptenlightenment/Vhm2a/*)

```
<!DOCTYPE html><html lang="en"><body><script>

var myArray = ['blue', 'green', 'orange', 'red'];

var myArrayLength = myArray.length; /* cache array length, to avoid unnecessary
                                       lookup */
var counter = 0; // setup counter

while (counter < myArrayLength) { // run if counter is less than array length
   console.log(myArray[counter]); // logs 'blue', 'green', 'orange', 'red'
   counter++; // add 1 to the counter
}

</script></body></html>
```

And now we loop from the end of the index to the beginning.

Live Code (*http://jsfiddle.net/javascriptenlightenment/DYcpX/*)

```
<!DOCTYPE html><html lang="en"><body><script>

var myArray = ['blue', 'green', 'orange', 'red'];

var myArrayLength = myArray.length;
while (myArrayLength--) {                /* if length is not zero, loop and
                                           subtract 1 */
   console.log(myArray[myArrayLength]); // logs 'red', 'orange', 'green', 'blue'
}

</script></body></html>
```

If you are wondering why I am not showing `for` loops here, it is because `while` loops have fewer moving parts and I believe they are easier to read.

CHAPTER 10

String()

Conceptual Overview of Using the String() Object

The String() constructor function is used to create string objects and string primitive values.

In the code below, I detail the creation of string values in JavaScript.

Live Code (*http://jsfiddle.net/javascriptenlightenment/deT8R/*)

```
<!DOCTYPE html><html lang="en"><body><script>

// create string object using the new keyword and the String() constructor
var stringObject = new String('foo');
console.log(stringObject); // logs foo {0 = 'f', 1 = 'o', 2 = 'o'}
console.log(typeof stringObject); // logs 'object'

// create string literal/primitive by directly using the String constructor
var stringObjectWithOutNewKeyword = String('foo'); // without new keyword
console.log(stringObjectWithOutNewKeyword); // logs 'foo'
console.log(typeof stringObjectWithOutNewKeyword); // logs 'string'

// create string literal/primitive (constructor leveraged behind the scene)
var stringLiteral = 'foo';
console.log(stringLiteral); // logs foo
console.log(typeof stringLiteral); // logs 'string'

</script></body></html>
```

String() Parameters

The String() constructor function takes one parameter: the string value being created. Below, we create a variable, stringObject, to contain the string value 'foo'.

```
<!DOCTYPE html><html lang="en"><body><script>

// create string object
var stringObject = new String('foo');

console.log(stringObject); // logs 'foo {0="f", 1="o", 2="o"}'

</script></body></html>
```

Note

Instances from the String() constructor, when used with the new keyword, produce an actual complex object. You should avoid doing this (using literal/primitive numbers) due to the potential problems associated with the typeof operator. The typeof operator reports complex string objects as 'object' instead of the primitive label ('string') you might expect. Additionally, the literal/primitive value is just faster to write and is more concise.

String() Properties and Methods

The string object has the following properties and methods (not including inherited properties and methods):

Properties (e.g., String.prototype;):

- prototype

Methods (e.g., String.fromCharChode();):

- fromCharCode()

String Object Instance Properties and Methods

String object instances have the following properties and methods:

Instance Properties (e.g., var myString = 'foo'; myString.length;):

- constructor
- length

Instance Methods (e.g., var myString = 'foo'; myString.toLowerCase

- charAt()
- charCodeAt()
- concat()
- indexOf()
- lastIndexOf()
- localeCompare()
- match()
- quote()
- replace()
- search()
- slice()
- split()
- substr()
- substring()
- toLocaleLowerCase()
- toLocaleUpperCase()
- toLowerCase()
- toString()
- toUpperCase()
- valueOf()

CHAPTER 11

Number()

Conceptual Overview of Using the Number() Object

The Number() constructor function is used to create numeric objects and numeric primitive values.

In the code below, I detail the creation of numeric values in JavaScript.

Live Code (http://jsfiddle.net/javascriptenlightenment/QJNRA/)

```
<!DOCTYPE html><html lang="en"><body><script>

// create number object using the new keyword and the Number() constructor
var numberObject = new Number(1);
console.log(numberObject); // logs 1
console.log(typeof numberObject) // logs 'object'

// create number literal/primitive using the number constructor without new
var numberObjectWithOutNew = Number(1); // without using new keyword
console.log(numberObjectWithOutNew); // logs 1
console.log(typeof numberObjectWithOutNew) // logs 'number'

// create number literal/primitive (constructor leveraged behind the scene)
var numberLiteral = 1;
console.log(numberLiteral); // logs 1
console.log(typeof numberLiteral); // logs 'number'


</script></body></html>
```

Integers and Floating-Point Numbers

Numbers in JavaScript are typically written as either integer values or floating point values. In the code below, I create a primitive integer number and a primitive floating point number. This is the most common usage of number values in JavaScript.

Live Code (*http://jsfiddle.net/javascriptenlightenment/c4TVQ/*)

```
<!DOCTYPE html><html lang="en"><body><script>

var integer = 1232134;
console.log(integer); // logs '1232134'

var floatingPoint = 2.132;
console.log(floatingPoint); // logs '2.132'

</script></body></html>
```

Note

In JavaScript, a numeric value can be a hexadecimal value (*http://live page.apple.com/*) or octal value (*http://en.wikipedia.org/wiki/Octal*), but this is typically not done.

Number() Parameters

The `Number()` constructor function takes one parameter: the numeric value being created. Below, we create a number object for the value 456 called `numberOne`.

Live Code (*http://jsfiddle.net/javascriptenlightenment/aHbNY/*)

```
<!DOCTYPE html><html lang="en"><body><script>

var numberOne = new Number(456);

console.log(numberOne); // logs '456{}'

</script></body></html>
```

Note

Instances from the `Number()` constructor, when used with the new keyword, produce a complex object. You should avoid creating number values using the `Number()` constructor (use literal/primitive numbers) due to the potential problems associated with the `typeof` operator. The `typeof` operator reports number objects as `'object'` instead of the primitive label (`'number'`) you might expect. The literal/primitive value is just more concise.

Number() Properties

The `Number()` object has the following properties:

Properties (e.g., `Number.prototype;`):

- `MAX_VALUE`
- `MIN_VALUE`
- `NaN`
- `NEGATIVE_INFINITY`
- `POSITIVE_INFINITY`
- `prototype`

Number Object Instance Properties and Methods

Number object instances have the following properties and methods:

Instance Properties (e.g., `var myNumber = 5; myNumber.constructor;`):

- `constructor`

Instance Methods (e.g., `var myNumber = 1.00324; myNumber.toFixed();`):

- `toExponential()`
- `toFixed()`
- `toLocaleString()`
- `toPrecision()`
- `toString()`
- `valueOf()`

CHAPTER 12

Boolean()

Conceptual Overview of Using the Boolean() Object

The Boolean() constructor function can be used to create boolean objects, as well as boolean primitive values, that represent either a true or a false value.

In the code below, I detail the creation of boolean values in JavaScript.

Live Code (*http://jsfiddle.net/javascriptenlightenment/wSqVc/*)

```
<!DOCTYPE html><html lang="en"><body><script>

// create boolean object using the new keyword and the Boolean() constructor
var myBoolean1 = new Boolean(false); // using new keyword
console.log(typeof myBoolean1); // logs 'object'

/* create boolean literal/primitive by directly using the number constructor
without new */
var myBoolean2 = Boolean(0); // without new keyword
console.log(typeof myBoolean2); // logs 'boolean'

// create boolean literal/primitive (constructor leveraged behind the scene)
var myBoolean3 = false;
console.log(typeof myBoolean3); // logs 'boolean'
console.log(myBoolean1, myBoolean2, myBoolean3); // logs false false false

</script></body></html>
```

Boolean() Parameters

The Boolean() constructor function takes one parameter to be converted to a boolean value (i.e., true or false). Any valid JavaScript value that is not 0, -0, null, false, NaN, undefined, or an empty string(""), will be converted to true. Below, we create two boolean object values. One true, one false.

Live Code (*http://jsfiddle.net/javascriptenlightenment/4TEtb/*)

```
<!DOCTYPE html><html lang="en"><body><script>

// parameter passed to Boolean() = 0 = false, thus foo = false
var foo = new Boolean(0)
console.log(foo);

// parameter passed to Boolean() = Math = true, thus bar = true
var bar = new Boolean(Math)
console.log(bar);

</script></body></html>
```

Note

Instances from the Boolean() constructor, when used with the new keyword, produce an actual complex object. You should avoid creating boolean values using the Boolean() constructor (instead, use literal/primitive numbers) due to the potential problems associated with the typeof operator. The typeof operator reports boolean objects as 'object', instead of the primitive label ('boolean') you might expect. Additionally, the literal/primitive value is just faster to write.

Boolean() Properties and Methods

The Boolean() object has the following properties:

Properties (e.g., Boolean.prototype;):

- prototype

Boolean Object Instance Properties and Methods

Boolean object instances have the following properties and methods:

Instance Properties (e.g., `var myBoolean = false; myBoolean.constructor;`):

- `constructor`

Instance Methods (e.g., `var myNumber = false; myBoolean.toString();`):

- `toSource()`
- `toString()`
- `valueOf()`

Non-Primitive False Boolean Objects Convert to true

A `false` boolean object (as opposed to a primitive value) created from the `Boolean()` constructor is an object, and objects convert to `true`. Thus, when creating a `false` boolean object via the `Boolean()` constructor, the value itself converts to `true`. Below, I demonstrate how a `false` boolean object is always "truthy."

Live Code (*http://jsfiddle.net/javascriptenlightenment/K7qtj/*)

```
<!DOCTYPE html><html lang="en"><body><script>

var falseValue = new Boolean(false);

console.log(falseValue); // we have a false boolean object, but objects are truthy

if (falseValue) { // boolean objects, even false boolean objects, are truthy
    console.log('falseValue is truthy');
}

</script></body></html>
```

If you need to convert a non-boolean value into a boolean, just use the `Boolean()` constructor without the `new` keyword and the value returned will be a primitive value instead of a boolean object.

Certain Things Are false, Everything Else Is true

It has already been mentioned, but is worth mentioning again because it pertains to conversions. If a value is 0, -0, null, false, NaN, undefined, or an empty string(""), it is false. Any value in JavaScript except the aforementioned values will be converted to true if used in a boolean context (i.e., if (true) {};).

Live Code (*http://jsfiddle.net/javascriptenlightenment/2aqGS/*)

```
<!DOCTYPE html><html lang="en"><body><script>

// all of these return a false boolean value
console.log(Boolean(0));
console.log(Boolean(-0));
console.log(Boolean(null));
console.log(Boolean(false));
console.log(Boolean(''));
console.log(Boolean(undefined));
console.log(Boolean(null));

// all of these return a true boolean value
console.log(Boolean(1789));
console.log(Boolean('false')); /* 'false' as a string is not false
                                  the boolean value */
console.log(Boolean(Math));
console.log(Boolean(Array()));

</script></body></html>
```

It's critical that you understand which JavaScript values are reduced to false so you are aware that all other values are considered true.

CHAPTER 13

Working with Primitive String, Number, and Boolean Values

Primitive/Literal Values Are Converted to Objects When Properties Are Accessed

Do not be mystified by the fact that string, number, and boolean literals can be treated like an object with properties [e.g., `true.toString()`]. When these primitive values are treated like an object by attempting to access properties, JavaScript will create a wrapper object from the primitive's associated constructor, so that the properties and methods of the wrapper object can be accessed. Once the properties have been accessed, the wrapper object is discarded. This conversion allows us to write code that would make it appear as if a primitive value was, in fact, an object. Truth be told, when it is treated like an object in code, JavaScript will convert it to an object so property access will work, and then back to a primitive value once a value is returned. The key thing to grok here is what is occurring, and that JavaScript is doing this for you behind the scenes.

String:

Live Code (*http://jsfiddle.net/javascriptenlightenment/kpfNk/*)

```
<!DOCTYPE html><html lang="en"><body><script>

// string object treated like an object
var stringObject = new String('foo');
console.log(stringObject.length); // logs 3
console.log(stringObject['length']); // logs 3

// string literal/primitive converted to an object when treated as an object
var stringLiteral = 'foo';
console.log(stringLiteral.length); // logs 3
```

```
console.log(stringLiteral['length']); // logs 3
console.log('bar'.length); // logs 3
console.log('bar'['length']); // logs 3

</script></body></html>
```

Number:

Live Code (*http://jsfiddle.net/javascriptenlightenment/sQXdE/*)

```
<!DOCTYPE html><html lang="en"><body><script>

// number object treated like an object
var numberObject = new Number(1.10023);
console.log(numberObject.toFixed()); // logs 1
console.log(numberObject['toFixed']()); // logs 1

// number literal/primitive converted to an object when treated as an object
var numberLiteral = 1.10023;
console.log(numberLiteral.toFixed()); // logs 1
console.log(numberLiteral['toFixed']()); // logs 1
console.log((1234).toString()); // logs '1234'
console.log(1234['toString']()); // logs '1234'

</script></body></html>
```

Boolean:

Live Code (*http://jsfiddle.net/javascriptenlightenment/dQMHs/*)

```
<!DOCTYPE html><html lang="en"><body><script>

// boolean object treated like an object
var booleanObject = new Boolean(0);
console.log(booleanObject.toString()); // logs 'false'
console.log(booleanObject['toString']()); // logs 'false'

// boolean literal/primitive converted to an object when treated as an object
var booleanLiteral = false;
console.log(booleanLiteral.toString()); // logs 'false'
console.log(booleanLiteral['toString']()); // logs 'false'
console.log((true).toString()); // logs 'true'
console.log(true['toString']()); // logs 'true'

</script></body></html>
```

Note

When accessing a property on a primitive number directly (not stored in a variable), you have to first evaluate the number before the value is treated as an object (e.g., `(1).toString();` or `1..toString();`). Why two dots? The first dot is considered a numeric decimal, not an operator for accessing object properties.

You Should Typically Use Primitive String, Number, and Boolean Values

The literal/primitive values that represent a string, number, or boolean are faster to write and are more concise in the literal form.

You should use the literal value because of this. Additionally, the accuracy of the `type of` operator depends upon how you create the value (literal versus constructor invocation). If you create a string, number, or boolean object, the `typeof` operator reports the type as an object. If you use literals, the `typeof` operator returns a string name of the actual value type (e.g., `typeof 'foo' // returns 'string'`).

In the code below, I demonstrate this fact.

Live Code (*http://jsfiddle.net/javascriptenlightenment/NYcnn/*)

```
<!DOCTYPE html><html lang="en"><body><script>

// string, number, and boolean objects
console.log(typeof new String('foo')); // logs 'object'
console.log(typeof new Number(1)); // logs 'object'
console.log(typeof new Boolean(true)); // logs 'object'

// string, number, and boolean literals/primitives
console.log(typeof 'foo'); // logs 'string'
console.log(typeof 1); // logs 'number'
console.log(typeof true); // logs 'boolean'

</script></body></html>
```

If your program depends upon the `typeof` operator to identify string, number, or boolean values in terms of those primitive types, you should avoid the `String()`, `Number()`, and `Boolean()` constructors.

CHAPTER 14

Null

Conceptual Overview of Using the null Value

You can use null to explicitly indicate that an object property does not contain a value. Typically, if a property is set up to contain a value, but the value is not available for some reason, the value null should be used to indicate that the reference property has an empty value.

Live Code (*http://jsfiddle.net/javascriptenlightenment/PBq4y/*)

```
<!DOCTYPE html><html lang="en"><body><script>

// the property foo is waiting for a value, so we set its initial value to null
var myObjectObject = {foo: null};

console.log(myObjectObject.foo); //logs 'null'

</script></body></html>
```

Note

Don't confuse null with undefined. undefined is used by JavaScript to tell you that something is missing. null is provided so you can determine when a value is expected but just not available yet.

typeof Returns null Values as "object"

For a variable that has a value of null, the typeof operator returns 'object'. If you need to verify a null value, the ideal solution would be to see if the value you are after is equal to null. Below, we use the === operator to specifically verify that we are dealing with a null value.

```
<!DOCTYPE html><html lang="en"><body><script>

var myObject = null;

console.log(typeof myObject); // logs 'object', not exactly helpful
console.log(myObject === null); // logs true, only for a real null value

</script></body></html>
```

 Note

When verifying a null value, always use === because == does not distinguish between null and undefined.

CHAPTER 15

Undefined

Conceptual Overview of the undefined Value

The undefined value is used by JavaScript in two slightly different ways.

The first way it's used is to indicate that a declared variable (e.g., var foo) has no *assigned value*. The second way it's used is to indicate that an object property you're trying to access is not *defined* (i.e., it has not even been named), and is not found in the prototype chain.

Below, I examine both usages of undefined by JavaScript.

Live Code (*http://jsfiddle.net/javascriptenlightenment/kGhrK/*)

```
<!DOCTYPE html><html lang="en"><body><script>

var initializedVariable; // declare variable

console.log(initializedVariable); // logs undefined
console.log(typeof initializedVariable); /* confirm that JavaScript returns
                                            undefined */

var foo = {};

console.log(foo.bar); // logs undefined, no bar property in foo object
console.log(typeof foo.bar); // confirm that JavaScript returns undefined

</script></body></html>
```

Note

It is considered good practice to allow JavaScript alone to use undefined. You should never find yourself setting a value to undefined, as in *foo = undefined*. Instead, null should be used if you are specifying that a property or variable value is not available.

JavaScript ECMAScript 3 Edition (and Later) Declares the undefined Variable in the Global Scope

Unlike previous versions, JavaScript ECMAScript 3 Edition (and later) has a global variable called undefined declared in the global scope. Because the variable is declared, and not assigned a value, the undefined variable is set to undefined.

Live Code (*http://jsfiddle.net/javascriptenlightenment/MhRKB/*)

```
<!DOCTYPE html><html lang="en"><body><script>

// confirm that undefined is a property of the global scope
console.log(undefined in this); // logs true

</script></body></html>
```

CHAPTER 16

Math Function

Conceptual Overview of the Built-In Math Object

The Math object contains static properties and methods for mathematically dealing with numbers or providing mathematical constants (e.g., Math.PI;). This object is built into JavaScript, as opposed to being based on a Math() constructor that creates math instances.

Note
It might seem odd that Math starts with a capitalized letter since you do not instantiate an instance of a Math object. Do not be thrown off by this. Simply be aware that JavaScript sets this object up for you.

Math Properties and Methods

The Math object has the following properties and methods:

Properties (e.g., Math.PI;):

- E
- LN2
- LN10
- LOG2E
- LOG10E
- PI

- SQRT1_2
- SQRT2

Methods (e.g., `Math.random();`):

- `abs()`
- `acos()`
- `asin()`
- `atan()`
- `atan2()`
- `ceil()`
- `cos()`
- `exp()`
- `floor()`
- `log()`
- `max()`
- `min()`
- `pow()`
- `random()`
- `round()`
- `sin()`
- `sort()`
- `tan()`

Math Is Not a Constructor Function

The `Math` object is unlike the other built-in objects that are instantiated. `Math` is a one-off object created to house static properties and methods, ready to be used when dealing with numbers. Just remember, there is no way to create an instance of `Math`, as there is no constructor.

Math Has Constants You Cannot Augment/Mutate

Many of the `Math` properties are constants (*http://en.wikipedia.org/wiki/Constant_%2528programming%2529*) that cannot be mutated. Since this is a departure from the mutable nature of JavaScript, these properties are in all-caps (e.g., `Math.PI;`). Do not confuse these property constants for constructor functions due to the capitalization of their first letter. They are simply object properties that cannot be changed.

Note

User-defined constants are not possible in JavaScript 1.5, ECMAScript 3 Edition.

Review

The following points summarize what you should have learned during the reading of this book (and investigation of code examples). Read each summary, and if you don't understand what is being said, return to the topic in the book.

- An object is made up of named properties that store values.

- Most everything in JavaScript can act like an object. Complex values are, well, objects and primitive values can be treated like objects. This is why you may hear people say that everything in JavaScript is an object.

- Objects are created by invoking a constructor function with the new keyword, or by using a shorthand literal expression.

- Constructor functions are objects (Function() objects), thus, in JavaScript, objects create objects.

- JavaScript offers 9 native constructor functions: Object(), Array(), String(), Number(), Boolean(), Function(), Date(), RegExp(), and Error(). The String(), Number(), and Boolean() constructors are dual-purposed in providing a) primitive values and b) object wrappers when needed, so that primitive values can act like objects when so treated.

- The values null, undefined, "string", 10, true, and false are all primitive values, without an object nature unless treated like an object.

- When the Object(), Array(), String(), Number(), Boolean(), Function(), Date(), RegExp(), and Error() constructor functions are invoked using the new keyword, an object is created that is known as a "complex object" or "reference object."

- "string", 10, true, and false, in their primitive forms, have no object qualities until they are used as objects; then JavaScript, behind the scenes, creates temporary wrapper objects so that such values can act like objects.

- Primitive values are stored by value, and when copied, are literally copied. Complex object values, on the other hand, are stored by reference, and when copied, are copied by reference.

- Primitive values are equal to other primitive values when their values are equal, whereas complex objects are equal only when they reference the same value. That is: a complex value is equal to another complex value when they both refer to the same object.

- Due to the nature of complex objects and references, JavaScript objects have dynamic properties.

- JavaScript is mutable, which means that native objects and user-defined object properties can be manipulated at any time.

- Getting/setting/updating an object's properties is done by using dot notation or bracket notation. Bracket notation is convenient when the name of the object property being manipulated is in the form of an expression [e.g., `Array['prototype']` `['join'].apply()`].

- When referencing object properties, a lookup chain is used to first look at the object that was referenced for the property; if the property is not there, the property is looked for on the constructor function's `prototype` property. If it's not found there, because the prototype holds an object value and the value is created from the `Object()` constructor, the property is looked for on the `Object()` constructor's `prototype` property (`Object.prototype`). If the property is not found there, then the property is determined to be `undefined`.

- The Prototype lookup chain is how inheritance (a.k.a. prototypal inheritance) was designed to be accomplished in JavaScript.

- Because of the object property lookup chain (a.k.a. prototypal inheritance), all objects inherit from `Object()` simply because the `prototype` property is, itself, an `Object()` object.

- JavaScript functions are first-class citizens: functions are objects with properties and values.

- The `this` keyword, when used inside a function, is a generic way to reference the object containing the function.

- The value of `this` is determined during runtime based on the context in which the function is called.

- Used in the global scope, the `this` keyword refers to the global object.

- JavaScript uses functions as a way to create a unique scope.

- JavaScript provides the global scope, and it's in this scope that all JavaScript code exists.

- Functions (specifically, encapsulated functions) create a scope chain for resolving variable lookups.

- The scope chain is set up based on the way code is written, not necessarily by the context in which a function is invoked. This permits a function to have access to the scope in which it was originally written, even if the function is called from a different context. This result is known as a closure.

- Function expressions and variables declared inside a function without using `var` become global properties. However, function statements inside of a function scope remain defined in the scope in which they are written.

- Functions and variables declared (without `var`) in the global scope become properties of the global object.

- Functions and variables declared (with `var`) in the global scope become global variables.

Conclusion

It's my hope that after reading this book, you will be equipped to either better understand your JavaScript library of choice, or better yet, be equipped to write your own JavaScript solutions. Either way this book alone was not written to be a definitive guide to the language. From here, I would recommend reading (or rereading) the following books so that the topics explained here may be reinforced from a different voice, and additional JavaScript topics may be examined and explored:

- *JavaScript: The Good Parts*, by Douglas Crockford (O'Reilly)
- *JavaScript Patterns*, by Stoyan Stefanov (O'Reilly)
- *Object-Oriented JavaScript*, by Stoyan Stefanov (Packt Publishing)
- *Professional JavaScript for Web Developers*, by Nicholas C. Zakas (Wiley/Wrox)
- *High Performance JavaScript*, by Nicholas C. Zakas (O'Reilly)

Index

Symbols

( ) (parentheses)
    invoking methods, 36
    parentheses operator, 51
        invoking function expressions, 61
. (dot)
    dot notation, getting setting object proper-
        ties with, 33
= (equals sign)
    == (equal to) operator, null values and, 128
    === (identity) operator
        comparison of primitive values, 17
        comparisons of complex objects, 21
        verifying null values, 127
[ ] (square brackets)
    bracket chaining to access encapsulated ar-
        rays, 108
    bracket notation, getting/setting object prop-
        erties, 34

A

alert( ) function, 70
anonymous functions, 61
    passing to and returning from other func-
        tions, 63
    self-invoking anonymous function state-
        ments, 62

apply( ) method, 60
    using to control value of this keyword, 78
arguments array, 58
arguments object, 56
    callee property, 56
    length property, 57
Array( ) constructor, 8, 103–110
    Array( ) object properties and methods, 104
    complex values, 19
    creating arrays, 105
    creating instance with its own instance prop-
        erty, 27
    instantiating instance using new operator, 11
    objects containing other complex objects, 33
    parameters, 104
    using Array( ) objects, conceptual overview,
        103
Array.prototype, 37, 95, 104
arrays
    adding and updating values in, 106
    array object instance properties and meth-
        ods, 105
    containing other arrays (multidimensional),
        108
    defining with predefined length, 107
    length versus index, 107
    looping over, backward and forward, 109
    setting length property, adding or removing
        values, 108

We'd like to hear your suggestions for improving our indexes. Send email to index@oreilly.com.

using Array( ) objects, conceptual overview,
103
associative arrays, mimicking with use of bracket notation, 36

B

block scope, nonexistent in JavaScript, 84
Boolean( ) constructor, 8, 119–122
    Boolean( ) object properties and methods,
120
    creation of literal/primitive and complex val-
ues, 14
    false boolean objects created from, conver-
sion to true, 121
    instantiating instance using new operator, 11
    literal values and, 12
    parameters, 120
    using Boolean object, conceptual overview,
119
    values converting to false and true values,
122
booleans
    as primitive or simple values, 13
    boolean primitive values behaving as objects,
18
    working with primitive boolean values, 124
bracket chaining, 108
bracket notation, getting/setting object properties, 34
built-in object constructors, 8

C

call( ) method, 60
    using to control value of this keyword, 77
callee property, arguments object, 56
chaining, object, 36
closures, 52
    caused by scope chain, 88
code examples in this book, xii
complex objects
    containing most JavaScript values as proper-
ties, 31
    encapsulating in programmatically benefi-
cial way, 32
complex values, 19
    storing and copying in JavaScript, 20
    typeof operator used on, 22
composite values (see complex values)

console.log function, xii
constants, 133
constructor functions, 103
    (see also individual constructor names)
    constructing and returning object instances,
6
    creating shorthand/literal values from, 12
    defined, 3
    instance created from, having its own in-
stance properties, 27
    instances created from, linkage to construc-
tor's prototype property, 94
    instantiating using new operator, 10–12
    native or built-in object constructors, 8
    objects instantiated by, constructor property
and, 24
    prototype object, 37
    review, 135
    same prototype inheritance in user-defined
and native constructors, 99
    this keyword in prototype method, 80
    user-defined, using this keyword in, 79
    user-defined/non-native object constructors,
9
    verifying object as instance of, 26
constructor property, 24
    boolean object instances, 121
    default, removal by replacing default proto-
type property, 96
    number object instances, 117
    tracing link from object to prototype object
it inherits, 94
    use on user-defined constructor functions,
26
context, function calls, this keyword and, 75
copying
    complex values, 20
    primitive values, 16

D

Date( ) constructor, 8
    complex values, 19
    creating date objects, 12
    instantiating instance using new operator, 11
decodeURI( ) function, 68
decodeURIComponent( ) function, 68
delete operator, 36
DOM (Document Object Model), 42

user-defined, non-native object constructor functions, 9
verifying as instance of a constructor function, 26
verifying that property is not from prototype chain, 39

P

parseFloat( ) function, 68
parseInt( ) function, 68
Person( ) custom constructor, 9
    leveraging prototype inheritance, 100
    using this keyword in, 79
primitive values, 13
    constructor properties pointing to constructor functions, 26
    equal by value, 17
    not objects, 15
    number, 115
    returning from Boolean( ) constructor, 121
    review, 135
    storing and copying in JavaScript, 16
    string, 111
    string, number, and boolean, behaving as objects, 18
    typeof operator used on, 22
    working with string, number, and boolean values, 123–125
        reasons to use primitive values, 125
properties
    complex objects, 31
    deleting object properties, 36
    dynamic properties allowing for mutable objects, 23
    dynamic properties of complex objects, 22
    enumerating object properties with for in loop, 40
    getting/setting for objects using dot or bracket notation, 33
    global, head object versus, 68
    instance, 27
    null value for object property, 127
    Object( ) instance properties, 47
    Object( ) object, 47
    objects as containers for, 2
    undefined object property, 129
    using in operator to check if object contains a property, 39

verifying object property is not from prototype chain, 39
property names, specified as strings, 48
propertyIsEnumerable( ) method, 47
__proto__ property, 37, 94
prototypal inheritance, 6, 136
prototype chain
    conceptual overview, 91
    Object.prototype as last stop, 95
    returning first property match found, 96
prototype property, 37, 91–101, 136
    all objects inheriting from Object.prototype, 49
    Array object, 104
    boolean object, 120
    constructor, linkage to instances created from constructor function, 94
    creating inheritance chains, 101
    on all Function( ) instances, 93
    Function.prototype, 53
    importance of, 92
    latest value for instances inheriting properties from, 97
    number object, 117
    as Object( ) object, 93
    Object.prototype, 47
    replacement with new object, not updating former instances, 98
    replacement with new object, removing default constructor property, 96
    string objects, 112
    this keyword inside prototype method, 80

R

recursion, 64
references
    to head object, 70
    to object properties, resolving, 37
RegExp( ) constructor, 8
    complex values, 19
    instantiating instance using new operator, 11
return keyword, canceling function execution, 58

S

scope, 83–89
    determination during function definition, not invocation, 87

Colophon

The animal on the cover of *JavaScript Enlightenment* is a Eurasian eagle owl (*Bubo bubo*), one of the largest species of owl in the world. Its habitat ranges from the dense forests of western Europe to the mountains of Asia, and from frigid Scandinavian fjords to the deserts of Saharan Africa and the Middle East.

The eagle owl is an imposing bird of prey with a large facial disc (the feathers surrounding the eyes) and bright orange eyes. It stands over 2 feet tall, with a wingspan up to 6 feet across. Along with its size, the dark vertical stripes on its feathers, a mottled white pattern on the breast, and prominent ear tufts make the eagle owl easy to identify.

This owl hunts by watching for prey from a high perch. When it spots a rabbit or other small mammal, it swoops in swiftly and low to the ground to capture prey with its large talons. Eagle owls can also pluck birds out of the air or plunge into water to grab a fish.

The eagle owl prefers to build nests on rocky ledges, crevices on the face of a cliff, or in the shelter of a cave entrance. A typical brood contains one to four owlets who are born in mid-to-late winter and grow quickly—by early spring, they are too large to remain in the nest. The female will continue to feed and protect her offspring even after they leave the nest, until they are able to hunt on their own in the fall.

The eagle owl can be seen soaring on thermal updrafts or flying with shallow wing beats and long glides, a pattern of flight more similar to the red-tailed hawk than other owl species. Eagle owls can be ferocious, especially when feeding and tending to their young, and have been known to fight other large birds of prey (such as golden eagles or peregrine falcons). When threatened, an eagle owl will puff out its chest and ear tufts to make itself seem larger.

The cover image is from *Meyers Lexikon*. The cover font is Adobe ITC Garamond. The text font is Adobe Minion Pro; the heading font is Adobe Myriad Condensed; and the code font is Dalton Maag's Ubuntu Mono.

Get even more for your money.

Join the O'Reilly Community, and register the O'Reilly books you own. It's free, and you'll get:

- $4.99 ebook upgrade offer
- 40% upgrade offer on O'Reilly print books
- Membership discounts on books and events
- Free lifetime updates to ebooks and videos
- Multiple ebook formats, DRM FREE
- Participation in the O'Reilly community
- Newsletters
- Account management
- 100% Satisfaction Guarantee

Signing up is easy:

1. **Go to: oreilly.com/go/register**
2. **Create an O'Reilly login.**
3. **Provide your address.**
4. **Register your books.**

Note: English-language books only

To order books online:
oreilly.com/store

For questions about products or an order:
orders@oreilly.com

To sign up to get topic-specific email announcements and/or news about upcoming books, conferences, special offers, and new technologies:
elists@oreilly.com

For technical questions about book content:
booktech@oreilly.com

To submit new book proposals to our editors:
proposals@oreilly.com

O'Reilly books are available in multiple DRM-free ebook formats. For more information:
oreilly.com/ebooks

Spreading the knowledge of innovators   oreilly.com

PR

CPSIA information can be obtained at www.ICGtesting.com
Printed in the USA
BVOW030954010413

316970BV00005B/71/P